The

BIG
TEXAS
STEAK
HOUSE
COOKBOOK

The BIG TEXAS STEAK HOUSE COOKBOOK

HELEN THOMPSON AND JANICE SHAY

photography by ROBERT PEACOCK

PELICAN PUBLISHING COMPANY
Gretna 2011

The word "Pelican" and the depiction of a pelican are trademarks
of Pelican Publishing Company, Inc., and are registered in the
U.S. Patent and Trademark Office.

ISBN-13: 978-1-58980-878-2

Printed in Singapore

Published by Pelican Publishing Company, Inc.
1000 Burmaster Street, Gretna, Louisiana 70053

Produced by Pinafore Press / Janice Shay

Recipe consultant, June Naylor
Editors, Laura Clark and Sarah Jones
Design assistant, Angela Rojas
Indexer, Sara LeVere

Recipes, pages 106, 114, from *Reata: Legendary Texas Cuisine* by Mike Micallef, photography by
Laurie Smith, copyright © 2009 by Michael Micallef. Used by permission of Ten Speed Press,
an imprint of the Crown Publishing Group, a division of Random House, Inc.

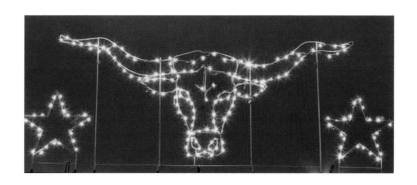

This book is dedicated to the wonderful owners, managers, and chefs who contributed their time and recipes. This is their book, as much as it is ours. —J.S.

To Charles, a meat enthusiast —H.T.

CONTENTS

Calling yourself a Texan is a bold statement. Texas is a big state and we Texans are known for our big appetite for all things beef—and the big ranches that produce this beef. After all, Texas is where the modern day ranching industry began over 100 years ago on the Chisholm Trail, a legendary cattle drive route starting at the tip of Texas on the Rio Grande and leading to the markets and railheads north to Kansas. The Fort Worth Stockyards was a stopping-off point for cowboys to rest their bones, get a hot bath, some whiskey and—most important— a big steak. Just as the cowboys coming off the trail yearned for a big juicy steak, our appetite for beef now is as big and strong as it has ever been, and doesn't seem to be diminishing. Although times have changed in the last hundred years, our appetite for all things beef is still as strong as ever—and getting stronger. Cooking with beef has come a long way, but it also remains unchanged in many ways. From our humble beginnings, Texas has grown into a formidable force in world cuisine and beef has played a major role in this. You can still find steaks cooked in the old-time traditions of the chuckwagon cooks today in such landmark places as Perini Ranch in Buffalo Gap or cooked in ultra-modern 1200-degree broilers. And you can find a lot more.

The restaurants and talented chefs featured in this book are as legendary as the state they cook in and hail from. The cooking methods and styles used today are as varied and wide as Texas itself. On our Southern border you might find red chile-cheese enchiladas on top of a chargrilled ribeye steak; or in the hill country, a thick juicy porterhouse crusted with a maple rub and grilled over an open flame; or in the panhandle of west Texas, a perfectly pepper-crusted smoked beef tenderloin; or in the stockyards of Fort Worth, a simple chicken fried steak with perfect cream gravy. Today's Texas steakhouses are as unique as the cooking methods and the chefs that run them. One thing is for sure: No matter where you go in Texas, beef is still the king!

Grady Spears, at Grady's Restaurant

INTRODUCTION

Welcome to the world of Texas beef. Texans are proud of many things—and rightly so. California may claim to have the most vegetarians (we'll give them that), Chicago may have better pizzas (it's arguable), but when it comes to steaks, there just ain't no other dog in this hunt. For reasons that go all the way back to the Chisolm Trail and the Fort Worth Stockyards, Texans own the bragging rights to who has the best beef. Billions of pounds of beef are produced annually here, and in most parts, cattle ranches and auctions are as thick as fleas on a dog.

In almost any county, town, hamlet, or roadside stop, there is an establishment that bills itself as a steakhouse. The simple reason for this is that Texans do not like to be far from their favorite fare. The restaurant doesn't need to be pretty—the quality of the cutlery don't matter as much as the cookin', as my grandmother would say. All it needs each day to attract long lines of hungry customers is to slap a fresh, thick, juicy slab of Texas-raised beef, grilled to perfection, on your table. Almost every country in the world boasts a restaurant named "Texas Steakhouse" or some version thereof—proof, if you didn't already know it, that news about the quality of Texas steaks has gone global.

Cowboys and cattle are seamlessly knit into an iconic image of Texas. Cattle ranching has been a way of life here for more than 100 years. What most people don't realize is that it is still a way of life all over Texas. The Texas Department of Agriculture recognizes almost 3,900 farms and ranches in 222 counties across Texas as having more than a century of continuous operation. Collectively, Texas has 150,000 ranchers, cattlemen and dairy farmers, which accounts for 15% of the nation's one million beef and dairy producers. All 254 Texas counties produce beef, and 45 counties have dairy herds of 500 head or more. Got all that? Now you know why Texans like to talk big—they ain't just whistlin' Dixie.

Naturally, we can't be the country's leading producer of beef and not love the stuff. We do—we absolutely do!—and we like to tell you about it. Don't try to convince us that steak's not good for us, muttering about "cholesterol" and "fat," and "but have you thought about the calories" as we cut

The steak dinner at right was photographed in the lobby of the Stockyards Hotel, a hotel that dates from 1907.

into that first juicy bite of a T-bone. If I have to stop eating to remind you that beef has eight times more vitamin B12, six times more zinc, and two and a half times more iron than that skinless chicken breast you just ordered, it just might ruin my dinner. I'll be happy to inform you, though, that beef is a natural nutrient-rich food, containing significant amounts of zinc, phosphorus, selenium and vitamin B12. In fact, if you'd like to have the energy to spend an extra hour at the gym, I would advise you to try a steak someday soon!

But I digress. Let me take you back to the origins of Texas beef. By 1854, as Harper's Weekly reported at that time, the most popular meal in America from coast to coast was steak. By the Civil War, Americans ate twice as much beef as Englishmen. Supplying the demand for these quantities of beef became a problem and more spacious grazing land was sought. The focus turned to the burgeoning West, and Texas not only had the wide open ranges, it had the cattle—wild cattle that had been imported and abandoned by the Spanish in Texas. These cattle were captured and became domesticated, after a couple of generations, as the famous Texas Longhorns.

Our image of the Texas cowboy was born on the great trail drives from the end of the Civil War to the mid-1880s. In that brief period of time, almost 10,000,000 cows walked the trails from Texas to the railheads of Kansas and Missouri. Many trail drives pushed as far as Wyoming, and even into Canada. The 700-mile journey from San Antonio to the stockyards of Abilene and beyond, moving at a rate of about a dozen miles a day, was called the Chisolm Trail. Compared to earlier efforts to move 50 or 100 head of cattle to market from Georgia or Ohio, these Texas herds numbered in the thousands. In 1867, a man named O. W. Wheeler and his partners used the Chisholm Trail to bring a herd of 2,400 steers from Texas to Abilene. This herd was the first of an estimated 5,000,000 head of Texas cattle to reach Kansas over the Chisholm Trail.

The cowboys who made the cattle drives would have a limited variety of food on the trail, but they made the best of it. Chuckwagon "coosies" (cooks) served up foods that still exist on Southern menus—biscuits, stews, chili, jerky, and anything they could scare up along the trail went into the pot. Longhorn was a tough meat, so the coosie had to pound it until tender, then dredged it in flour and fried it up in a Dutch oven. We know this as chicken fried steak—poor folks' food that remains a belly-filling favorite.

"The Texans are perhaps the best at the actual cowboy work. They are absolutely fearless riders and understand well the habit of the half-wild cattle, being unequaled in those most trying times when, for instance, the cattle are stampeded by a thunderstorm at night; while in the use of the rope they are only excelled by the Mexicans."

—Theodore Roosevelt, 1885

Trail drivers quickly realized that Fort Worth was situated at an ideal geographic spot to rest and re-supply before heading north across the Red River and into dangerous Indian country. Because the number of cattle driven through this town grew quickly, it soon became necessary to create a system of pens for holding the cattle before they headed north. What we know as the Fort Worth Stockyards was not the original location for this herding. When trail drivers needed to move the herds via railroads in the late 1800s, the best place to put this railway was a couple miles north of town, which is the current location of the Historic Fort Worth Stockyards.

Fort Worth became known as "The City Where the West Begins" and the stockyards were designated

a National Historic District in 1976, a hundred years after the arrival of the railroad. One of the oldest restaurants still serving in the stockyards is the Star Cafe, dating from the early 1900s. Daily, visitors can still see longhorns driven down Exchange Street, watch gun-toting cowboys roam the streets and alleyways, and visit many of the same businesses and hotels that have been in service for the last century.

Trail drives then and now: the trail drive above is staged daily in the Historic Fort Worth Stockyards.

This compilation of the recipes from the best Texas steakhouses is the first of its kind. Chefs Grady Spears and Tom Perini have spearheaded the effort to carry on the magnificent tradition of cowboy cooking, giving it their own contemporary flair. Kudos to them for keeping chuckwagon food alive and vital!

There is no shortage of cooking competitions statewide in which steak is the star, but the king of them all—the cookoff that can make or break a cook's career—is the annual Texas Steak Cookoff in Hico. The tiny town of Hico may be forever linked to the legend of Billy the Kid, but for one day each spring the community "Where Everybody is Somebody"—as their motto proudly proclaims—creates their own brand of Lone Star lore as chefs attempt to taste victory in the annual Texas Steak Cookoff, an epicurean event which has gained fame through its appearances on The Food Network and Everyday with Rachael Ray.

First held in 2004, the competition is three-tiered: celebrity chefs, professional chefs, and backyard cooks compete in their own category. Like this book, the Hico festival is an ode to steak, a celebration of Texans' steak lust, and a great way to find new ways to cook steaks.

Finally, a word about how this book was organized and how to use it. We compiled a list of the best recipes from the best steakhouses in Texas, relying on food writer and reviewer June Naylor of Dallas to choose the stars. It is by no means a complete list—we had only 200 pages to fill!—and I am sure that you can add your own favorites to the bunch. We had to make the difficult decision not to include the chain steakhouses, although many of them certainly serve great steaks.

Many of the chefs wrote directions for cooking one steak at a time, but if you're cooking for company, the rub recipes are ample enough to add a few more steaks to the grill without having to make a return trip to the grocery. Some businesses naturally didn't want to give away their secret rub recipes, but there are four listed *(pp. 160-161)* that should give you a good range of choices.

The chefs and restaurants mentioned are the best in a very large bunch of good steakhouses. Thankfully, these businesses are generally alive and well, having weathered the latest economic downturn by faithfully serving up what has long been a favorite food. It is my hope that steak will always be a way of life in Texas. It is part of our history—and we should never forget "who brung us to this dance." May you always find a steakhouse in any Texas town, big or small, and may these food traditions live on.

A few important icons: (shown clockwise from upper left): a Texas longhorn; the flag— symbol of Texas pride; legendary Southern hospitality; and the state dish—chili.

Cattlemen's Steak House, Fort Worth

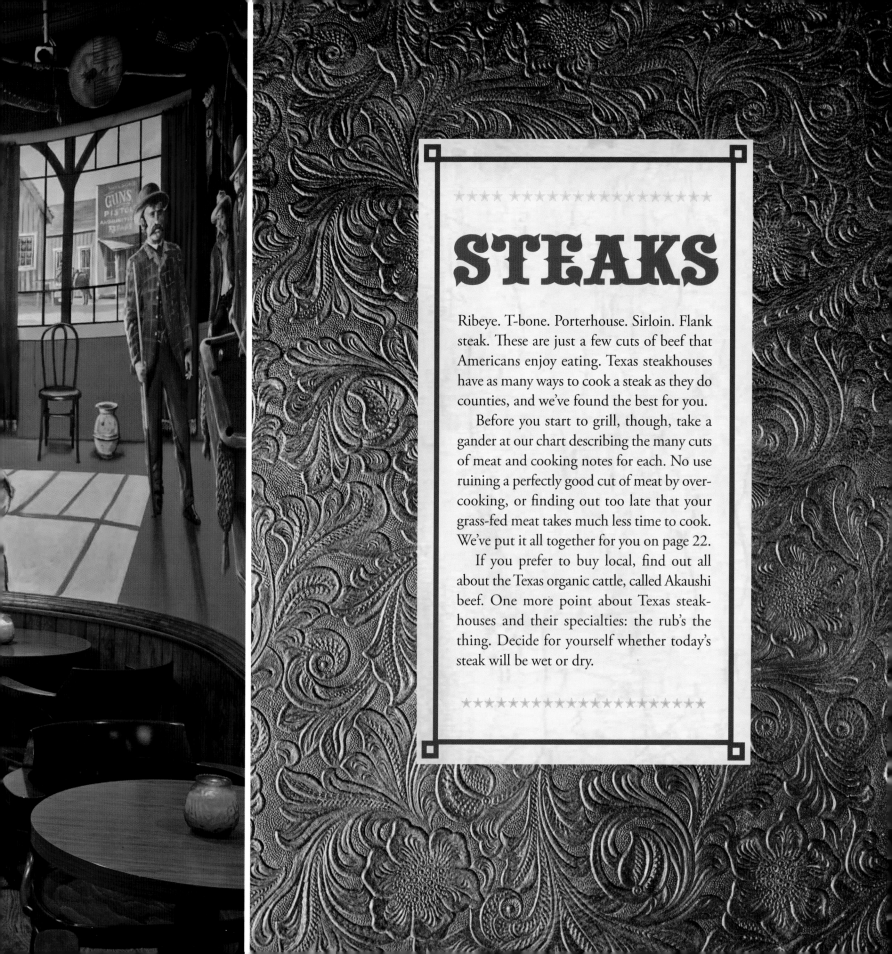

STEAKS

Ribeye. T-bone. Porterhouse. Sirloin. Flank steak. These are just a few cuts of beef that Americans enjoy eating. Texas steakhouses have as many ways to cook a steak as they do counties, and we've found the best for you.

Before you start to grill, though, take a gander at our chart describing the many cuts of meat and cooking notes for each. No use ruining a perfectly good cut of meat by over-cooking, or finding out too late that your grass-fed meat takes much less time to cook. We've put it all together for you on page 22.

If you prefer to buy local, find out all about the Texas organic cattle, called Akaushi beef. One more point about Texas steak-houses and their specialties: the rub's the thing. Decide for yourself whether today's steak will be wet or dry.

GRILLED TEXAS T-BONE WITH ROQUEFORT PORT COMPOUND BUTTER

Taste of Texas Restaurant, Houston

Serves 8

8 (20-ounce) T-Bone steaks
Coarse kosher salt
Cracked black pepper
Roquefort Port Compound Butter *(see recipe, p.158)*

Open since 1977, the Taste of Texas is a family owned and operated steakhouse. Visitors can pick out their own steaks at the restaurant's "butcher shop." To complete the traditional steakhouse experience, the Taste of Texas boasts an incredible collection of museum quality artifacts reflecting the heritage and history of Texas.

Salt the steaks and season them with cracked black pepper about an hour before they go on the grill to help lock in the natural juices and bring out the beefy flavor. Let steaks stand at room temperature during this time. The internal temperature of the steaks will rise a few degrees, which will decrease the amount of time they need to stay on the grill—and decrease the likelihood of drying out.

To prepare the grill, heat grill to high to burn off any residue on the grates. After about 7 to 8 minutes, scrub the grates with a stiff wire brush until any residue is gone. Once your grill is clean, heat one side to medium-high and the other to medium-low. If you use a charcoal grill, pile the charcoals mainly to one side, leaving a layer only 1 coal thick on the other side.

Next, oil the grill with a clean rag soaked with vegetable oil or grill spray. Using long-handled tongs, apply the oil to your grill grates just before grilling to prevent sticking, being careful not to squeeze any oil into the flames.

To make cross hatches—the proper grilling marks—on your steaks, place steaks over the medium-high portion of the grill. Rotate the steaks twice, flipping only once, and grill for about 2 minutes on each rotation. This produces beautiful perpendicular grill marks on both sides of the steak and sears the steak over the higher flame. Once you have nice grill marks, transfer the steaks to the medium-low heat side of the grill, close the cover and allow the steaks to slowly come up to the desired temperature.

Check for doneness. The grill cooks at the Taste of Texas Restaurant check for doneness by the "feel" of the steak, but the only foolproof method is to test the temperature of each steak with a meat thermometer. Start checking the T-bones after about 12 minutes.

Note: Make sure to insert the thermometer into the thickest portion of the steak, away from the bone. Allow the steak to come up to temperature, and remove the thermometer immediately. Leaving the thermometer in the grill will melt it.

Top with a pat of Roquefort Port Compound Butter *(recipe, p. 158),* and garnish with a sprig of thyme and your favorite side, and serve hot.

CHUCK
7-Bone Pot Roast
Arm Pot Roast
Blade Roast
Under Blade Pot Roast
Mock Tender Roast
Chuck Pot Roast
Chuck Eye Roast
Short Ribs
Top Blade Steak
Shoulder Petite Tender
Shoulder Tender Medallions

RIB
Ribeye steak
Ribeye roast
Rib Steak, small end
Back Ribs

SHORT LOIN
T-bone Steak
Porterhouse Steak
Tenderloin Roast (Filet Mignon)
Tenderloin Steak
Top Loin Steak

SIRLOIN
Sirloin Steak, round or flat bone
Top Sirloin Steak
Tri-tip Roast
Tri-tip Steak

ROUND
Round Steak
Eye Round Steak
Top and Bottom Round Steak
Tip Steak
Eye Round Roast
Bottom Round Roast
Boneless Rump Roast
Tip Roast

FLANK
Flank Steak

SHORT PLATE
Skirt Steak

FORESHANK
Brisket, flat half
Shank, cross cut

BRISKET
Brisket, whole
Brisket, point half

THE PERFECT CUT

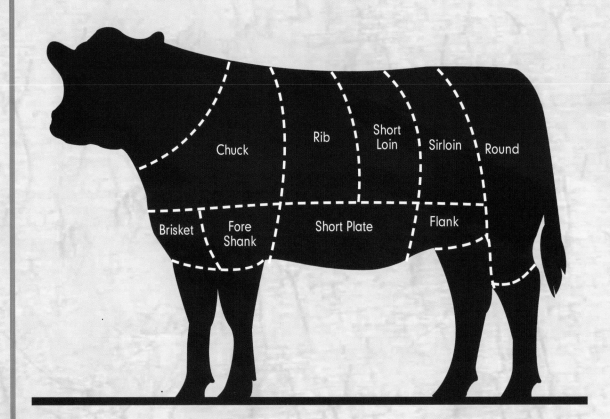

Chuck · Rib · Short Loin · Sirloin · Round · Brisket · Fore Shank · Short Plate · Flank

Backyard chefs revel in the mysteries of their cooking techniques; they credit their rituals with being the main reason a steak tastes great. But connoisseurs know that it's all about location, location, location. The part of the cow the meat comes from determines its tenderness, vigor, richness and personality. Although the meat industry is always searching for different ways to cut up a carcass to market to consumers, in general the cuts have remained the same.

What is meat, anyway? It's sheafs of muscle fibers wrapped in connective tissue that's enlivened with some fat (not too much, by the way). There's always a tug of war between flavor and tenderness, and the idyllic balance is a matter of personal choice. Fat equals tenderness. If that's what you are after, go for the cuts that emerge from the part of the cow that's doing the least amount of physical work, where the muscles are supple. These are located on the critter's midsection and back (tenderloins and rib eyes). Muscles that do the heavy lifting—in the legs, shoulders and chest—have been conditioned to be sturdy and pliant. Meat from these areas of the cow (clod, flank, round) will make up in flavor what it lacks in tenderness.

Remedy awaits, though: these cuts perk up considerably when pounded, marinated or dredged in flour.

Americans tend to worship steaks from the upper part of the cow, with the loin being the place where all's right on heaven and earth. Strip loins run a close second. Top sirloins are a good standby (although the same cannot be said for the sirloin tip, which is best in stews or roulades that don't depend on the meat for their flavor). The tenderloin, on the other hand, is indeed tender, but can be disappointingly characterless. For sheer eating pleasure that memories are made of, the ribeye rules.

A cut that's often overlooked by Americans, but beloved by the Japanese, is the tongue. Juicy and prodigiously flavorful, it is easily the equal to the ribeye in beefy charisma. There's also a rumor about

Butcher at Ranchman's Ponder Steakhouse

cuts known as "butcher's cuts," that are the domain of the in-the-know steak enthusiast. Skirt steak, hanger steak or flatiron steaks make up this category that purists might deride as trendy. The truth is that much depends on what a diner happens to like—and that the most reliable standard for excellence isn't, after all, the cut, but the source of the meat. A good way to start an argument is to challenge a believer in the infallibility of provenance: you're better off knowing the breed of cattle and how it was raised than by fussing over trivialities such as cut.

—H. T.

Trims & Tips

Whether you are grilling or cooking your steaks on the stove, these are some helpful cooking tips for common cuts of beef.

Ribeye steaks are great for grilling and smoking, as they are marbled with fat. Buy yours thick and sear it over medium-high heat.

Sirloin, New York Strip, and **Prime Rib** need a little salt, pepper, and olive oil.

Get your T-Bone, or **Porterhouse,** steak cut thick and sear it with the strip portion facing the hottest side of the grill and the tenderloins facing the cooler side.

Trim the fat on your **Brisket** to 1/4-inch thick. To test for tenderness, balance the brisket on your hand. If the ends droop slightly, it's not overcooked. A rigid brisket means tough, dry meat.

Filet Mignon is a tender cut, but it doesn't have the beefy flavor of other steaks, so use a good rub or marinade.

Although beefy and full-flavored, the **Flank Steak** is thin and cooks quickly. Carve it against the grain.

—J. S.

Temperature Guide for Steaks

130 DEGREES / rare to medium rare

135 to **145 DEGREES** / medium rare to medium

145 to **155 DEGREES** / medium well

155 DEGREES AND UP / well done

FLAMING TENDERLOIN

Hunter Brothers' H3 Ranch, Fort Worth

Serves 1

1 (9-ounce) center cut tenderloin
1/8 ounce coarse black pepper
1/8 ounce kosher salt

Flaming Butter
1 tablespoon dark rum
1 tablespoon butter

Located at the corners of Main and Exchange streets in the heart of Fort Worth's Historic Stockyards District, H3 Ranch serves lunch and dinner every day and breakfast on the weekends.

The live hickory wood grill serves up award-winning steaks, prime rib, and mighty tasty beef ribs.

To make the Flaming Butter, mix together dark rum and butter and set aside.

Thoroughly season tenderloin with salt and pepper mixture. Grill over live hickory wood grill to desired temperature. Remove steak from grill and dip into flaming butter.

Place back on hot grill to flame. Remove from grill and serve with your choice of classic side dishes, such as a baked potato and beans.

GRILL GUIDE

RARE / cook 4 minutes each side

MEDIUM RARE / cook 7 ½ minutes each side

MEDIUM / cook 11 minutes each side

MEDIUM WELL / cook 14 minutes each side

LINE CAMP RIBEYE

Line Camp Steakhouse, Tolar

Serves 6

6 (14-ounce) ribeye steaks
Salt
Pepper
Rub of your choice (see pp. 160-161)

Garlic Butter
1 stick butter, softened
4 cloves garlic, minced
2 tablespoons parsley flakes

Pinto Beans
1 pound pinto beans
1/2 red onion, julienned
2 to 4 whole jalapeños
4 slices uncooked bacon,
   cut in 1/2-inch pieces
Salt to taste

This is a destination restaurant with real Texas food, chuckwagon-style cooking, and true Southern comfort—Line Camp Steakhouse's strong suits. Award-winning steaks and hospitality keep folks coming back.

Featuring outdoor music on most weekends, Line Camp has a festive camp atmosphere that is as satisfying as the womderful food.

Line Camp cooks grill their steaks over an open fire using pecan wood. You may also use mesquite or coals. Make sure the grill is clean before you start to cook.

Salt and pepper the steaks and pat your choice of rub into both sides before you put it on the grill. Each time you flip the steaks, add a pat of garlic butter. When steaks are ready, top with another pat of garlic butter.

To prepare the pinto beans, thoroughly wash and soak beans in enough water to cover overnight. Drain beans and set aside. In a large pot, boil enough water to cover beans again. Cook until almost tender, about 30 to 45 minutes. Add all other ingredients and cook another 10 to 20 minutes, until tender.

To make the garlic butter, place all ingredients in a mixer and blend thoroughly.

PILONCILLA CRUSTED BEEF RIBEYE WITH A TEXAS CHEESE CHILE RELLENO

Grady's Restaurant, Fort Worth

Serves 4

4 (1 1/2 inches thick or 16-ounce) good
  quality ribeye steaks, well-marbled
4 tablespoons olive oil
3/4 cup piloncilla or light brown sugar
1/8 cup kosher salt
4 Poblano chilies, roasted, peeled,
  and deseeded
1 cup goat cheese, crumbled
1 cup Monterey Jack cheese, grated
2 tablespoons butter

Texas Pico
6 jalapeños, sliced
1 red onion, diced
6 green onions, thinly sliced
2 tomatoes, diced
2 bunches cilantro leaves, stems
  removed and minced
Juice of 2 limes
Kosher salt to taste

The name "chile relleno" literally means "stuffed chile" in Spanish. It is a perfect accompaniment to add spice to any ribeye.

Chef and owner Grady Spears serves up downhome, casual classics with a decidedly upscale flair, which suits his Fort Worth clientele perfectly. The dining room is sparsely and tastefully decorated with Western paintings, and the downstairs dining room is a private gallery featuring rotating exhibits of Texas art.

Preheat oven to 400 degrees.

On a platter large enough to hold all 4 steaks, coat each steak generously with the olive oil on both sides, and set aside for approximately 30 minutes to bring the steaks to room temperature.

In a bowl, combine the piloncilla and salt, mixing well. In a separate bowl, combine the goat cheese and jack cheese, mixing well. Place the roasted, peeled, and deseeded chilies on a sheet tray and fill each one with the cheese mixture.

Prepare a fire, or heat butter in a large skillet over medium-high heat. While the butter is melting, completely coat all sides of the steaks with the piloncilla rub, pressing the seasoning gently into the steaks. Sear steaks for 3 to 4 minutes on each side in hot butter, or until the seasoning forms a good crust. Remove from the skillet and place on a clean sheet tray. Place the seared steaks in the oven and cook for 6 to 8 minutes or until desired temperature is reached. Remove the steaks and let them rest.

While the steaks are resting, place the prepared chile rellenos in the oven and cook for 7 to 9 minutes or until the cheese in the rellenos has completely melted.

To make the Texas Pico, toss the jalapeños, onions, tomatoes, and cilantro in a bowl. Drizzle with lime juice, sprinkle with salt, and toss again. Let sit for about 15 minutes before serving.

To assemble, place 1 relleno on top of each steak, spoon on some pico, and serve immediately.

RANCHMAN'S ORIGINAL PAN-FRIED STEAK

Ranchman's Ponder Steakhouse, Ponder

Any steak of your choice
Bacon fat (optional)

Heat a large iron skillet or griddle to 375 degrees or set on medium-high heat. As the skillet is heating, season it with fat trimmed off the steak, or with bacon fat.

When the skillet is hot, add the steaks, turning only once until desired doneness is achieved.

Place on plate and spread Steak Butter *(see recipe, p. 158)* on top to melt. Serve with a baked potato or your choice of side dish.

TIP
Best cuts to pan fry are T-bone, porterhouse, ribeye, top loin, tenderloin, blade or tip steak.

Grace "Pete" Jackson opened Ranchman's Cafe in 1948 in Ponder, Texas, as a companion to Jackson's Store, a grocery that was next door to the landmark restaurant. The story goes that Pete served so many people from the counter of the grocery that she was forced to open a restaurant in order to accommodate all the business.

Even after selling the restaurant in 1992, Pete remained a regular, visiting several times a week, delighting customers and presiding over the dining room from her favorite chair.

New owner, Dave Ross, is shown in the photo at left.

BONE-IN STRIP WITH ASPARAGUS

Killen's Steakhouse, Pearland

Serves 1

Bone-in strip steak, (preferably Prime,
  dry-aged Allen Brother's beef)
Kosher salt
Black Pepper
1 bunch asparagus

Preheat broiler to 500 degrees.

Season steak with an equal mixture of black pepper and kosher salt. Lubricate a flat grill (you can also use a skillet) with rendered beef fat on high heat. Sear steak for 2 minutes on each side until meat turns black. Place the seared beef in a 500 degree broiler for approximately 6 minutes to achieve medium-rare doneness.

As the steak cooks, wash asparagus and shave the stalk to remove the purple part of the stalk. Blanch in boiling water for 10 to 15 minutes and serve hot. Garnish with a scoop of mashed potatoes and gravy.

As an upscale steakhouse right in the heart of Pearland—a suburb of Houston that can be found by driving 12 miles straight south on Telephone Road— Killen's is the only restaurant in town serving Kobe and Allen Brothers USDA Prime beef.

Chef Ronnie Killen returned to his hometown after training at Le Cordon Bleu and honing his culinary skills throughout the country. The property that is now Killen's Steakhouse was formerly an ice-house owned by his parents. Its low-key atmosphere is deceptive because some of the best food in Texas is served up daily.

BASEBALL CUT FILET

Silver Fox Steakhouse, Fort Worth

Serves 1

*This upscale steakhouse has four locations in Texas: Fort Worth, Grapevine, Frisco, and Richardson.
Silver Fox calls itself a USDA Prime beef emporium, offering only the finest Prime beef—one of the few exclusively Prime steakhouses in America.*

6, 8, or 10-ounce filet
4 tablespoons cracked black pepper
Pinch of fresh parsley

Rub pepper on both sides of steak prior to grilling. Cook steak over grill to desired temperature. Let rest for 5 minutes. Sprinkle with parsley and serve immediately.

. . . .

CATTLEMEN'S STEAKS

Cattlemen's Steak House, Fort Worth

Serves 1

Open and serving steaks since 1947, this staple of the Fort Worth Stockyards' restaurant herd never fails to delight. The big steaks have been compared to the size of Texas itself.

The restaurant includes wonderful murals depicting the Old West (see pp. 120 and 195), and the many different dining rooms are cozy and personal.

Steak of your choice, at least 1 to 1 1/2 inches thick
Salt
Pepper

To prepare, brush both sides of the steak with canola oil to prevent steaks from sticking to the grill, and sprinkle with salt and pepper. Cook over a charcoal grill.

THE 72-OUNCE STEAK CHALLENGE

Big Texan Steak Ranch, Amarillo

Serves 1

72-ounce top sirloin steak, or smaller cut of top sirloin
McCormick's Montreal Steak Seasoning

Au Jus
2 cups beef stock
Soy sauce, to taste
Worcestershire sauce, to taste
Black pepper to taste
1 clove garlic, crushed

Preheat the grill.

Sprinkle steak with seasoning just before you put it on the grill.

To make sure that the meat retains its juiciness, do not turn the steak too often. When the steak is done to your preferred temperature, serve it with au jus.

To make au jus, combine beef stock, soy sauce, Worcestershire sauce, black pepper, and garlic and warm in a small saucepan and over medium heat. Serve warm with the steak.

Owner Bob Lee says, "We are famous for the 72-ounce Steak Challenge. Our steaks, including the 72-ounce, are cold-aged for a minimum of 30 days to ensure that they are tender and flavorful. The 72-ounce steak is a top sirloin and though it is quite a show, we prepare and grill it the same way we do all of our wonderful cuts of steak. If you can eat it all, your steak is free."

Serving great steaks for half a century, the Big Texan Steak Ranch annually feeds almost a half million people from all over the world.

ROASTED GARLIC STUFFED BEEF TENDERLOIN WITH WESTERN PLAID HASH AND SYRAH DEMI-GLAZE

Lonesome Dove Western Bistro, Fort Worth

Serves 4

1 cup Australian Syrah wine
4 (8-ounce) beef tenderloin filets
2 cups veal stock *(see recipe, p. 40)*
4 cups peanut oil
2 russet potatoes
1/2 cup olive oil
1 clove garlic, crushed
10 garlic cloves, roasted *(recipe follows)*

1 cup red pepper, julienned
1 cup green cabbage, julienned
1 cup red cabbage, julienned
1 cup red onion, julienned
1/4 cup jalapeño, minced
Kosher salt and cracked black pepper, to taste

For the Syrah Demi-Glaze, bring ½ cup wine to a boil. Continue to boil until half the liquid has evaporated, then add veal stock, and again reduce by ⅔. Keep warm.

To make the Western Plaid Hash, heat peanut oil in a 4-quart saucepan over medium heat to 325 degrees. On a mandolin, or by hand, julienne the potatoes to ⅛-inch strips, and rinse in cool water to remove some starch.

When oil reaches 325 degrees, carefully drop potatoes in oil, stirring frequently. Cook for approximately 4 minutes, or until golden brown. Remove potatoes from oil, and drain on paper towels before seasoning with salt and pepper.

In a large iron skillet or a flat grill set on high heat, pour ¼ cup olive oil, and add peppers, cabbage, onions, and crushed garlic. Cook until cabbage is wilted, adding salt and pepper to taste. Add remainder of wine to cabbage mixture and simmer for 5 minutes. Reserve and keep warm.

To roast the garlic, use fresh cloves, unpeeled, and broken up into individual cloves. Place the cloves in a cast iron skillet or a heavy-bottomed sauté pan, and roast garlic over low heat for 20 to 30 minutes. Shake the pan occasionally to prevent the garlic from burning and to ensure even roasting. Garlic can also be roasted in the oven by placing the cloves in a 350 degree oven for 20 to 25 minutes, until lightly browned. When the garlic is done, it will be creamy, sweet, and soft enough to squeeze out of the clove. Garlic can be roasted ahead of time and reserved.

(Continued on the next page)

Opened in 2000, The Lonesome Dove Western Bistro, located in Fort Worth's Historic Stockyards District, has quickly acsended the ranks of great dining establishments, specifically because of chef / owner Tim Love's influence and expertise. A native Texan and Fort Worth's first chef invited to cook at the famed James Beard House in New York, Chef Love is known for his reverence for the food and culture of the American West—taking it to a new level of elegant sophistication.

Using a paring knife, make a small slit in the side of each tenderloin and stuff 1 clove of peeled, roasted garlic in each. Set aside.

Heat a large sauté pan on high and add ¼ cup olive oil.

Season filets by liberally rubbing salt and pepper onto each side of the steak. Place all 4 steaks in the pan, and sear on high for 1½ minutes on each side. Place pan in a 350 degree oven for 4 minutes, for medium-rare to medium steaks.

To plate, place potatoes in center of plate, and add the cabbage on top. Place tenderloin on top of the cabbage, and pour demi-glaze on top of the steak. Garnish with a seasonal green vegetable like grilled asparagus or green beans.

Veal Stock
(makes 2 quarts)

8 pounds veal bones (or veal and beef bones), cut into 2-inch chunks
2 medium onions, coarsely chopped
2 medium carrots, coarsely chopped
1 celery stalk, coarsely chopped
1 leek, coarsely chopped
2 large tomatoes, quartered, or 1/2 cup tomato paste
1 teaspoon whole peppercorns
2 bay leaves
2 sprigs fresh thyme
8 garlic cloves, smashed

Preheat the oven to 450 degrees.

Arrange the bones in a roasting pan large enough to hold them in a single layer. Roast in hot oven until dark golden brown, about 1½ hours, turning, to brown all sides.

Add all the remaining ingredients and allow to brown. Transfer the bones and vegetables to a large (10- to 12-quart) stockpot. Pour off the fat from the roasting pan, and deglaze the pan with 2 cups water, scraping up any particles that stick to the bottom of the pan. Pour into the stockpot with enough additional water to cover the ingredients by three inches.

Bring the water to a boil, reduce the heat and simmer, uncovered, 4 to 6 hours, skimming the foam as it accumulates on top and adding water as needed to keep the bones and vegetables covered at all times.

Strain the liquid into a clean pot, pressing down to extract all the juices. Reduce this mixture over medium heat, until 2 quarts remain. Cool and refrigerate in a covered container up to 3 days, discarding any hardened layer of fat before using or freezing.

Tim Love, Lonesome Dove Western Bistro

Organic Beef and Other Trends

Mention the adjective "organic" in tandem with "beef" and you've tapped into a hot button issue. Steak loyalists like their steak the way it's always been done. But a new generation of steak eaters has grown up dreaming dreams of good health, political correctness and the sanctity of nature. Anyone who's driven down a highway that passes by a feedlot and gotten a whiff of the powerfully acrid odor will know why the differences between old-fangled and new-fangled are so specific.

The choice of whether to seek out organic beef seems like a non-choice: would you like your sirloin from a cow that's been raised on certified organic pastures, has never received antibiotics or growth-promoting hormones, has been fed certified organic grains and grasses only and has had unrestricted access to the outdoors? That's a happy cow. Or, would you prefer to munch on a big rib eye from a cow that was implanted with a growth hormone (probably Ralgrow and Synovex) when it was three months old, later raised cheek by jowl with other cows in a feedlot where it was injected with growth hormones to be followed by hormone implants (such as Optaflexx) for muscle mass growth. As I said, the choice seems pretty clear.

But, maybe it's not so clear. Embedded in the discourse about organic beef is yet another argument: grain-fed or grass-fed? Which is better? As it happens, most grain-fed cattle are raised (or "finished") in feedlots. Grass-fed cows get to browse contentedly in pastures. The feedlot method is months quicker, and enthusiasts insist that the beef tastes better. It's marbled with fat, tastes meaty, and has a yielding succulence. Grass-fed steak is leaner—that's good for your arteries—but can sometimes taste like a salad.

Enterprising beef producers have tried to find a solution. The obvious ideal is to raise grain-fed cows on the range, and that's just what Dakota Beef 100% Organic, headquartered in Howard, South Dakota, does. But there is another faction—perhaps the hardcore—who believe that good beef is bred not fed. These are the ones who take specialization to the nth degree. Who else is better at that than the Japanese, whose black Wagyu cow produces the kind of meat legend is made of. Americans know it as Kobe beef (Kobe, Japan, is actually where the beef is from) and have heard all the rumors: the cattle are fed beer and have rice wine poured over their backs and massaged into their well-muscled flesh. Most importantly, though, the Wagyu possess a gene that produces a kind of fat that is mouth-wateringly fine.

You don't have to go to Japan to dine on this delicacy. It's expensive and can be found in expensive restaurants here. Texans have caught on, too, and are now raising their own kind of Wagyu—called Akaushi. The herd started with a mere eleven imported in 1994 by HeartBrand Beef to their South Texas ranch near Yoakum. It's now increased in size to 5,000 head, but the scarcity explains why you have to order your Akaushi steak days in advance from a steakhouse that offers it. The expense is a problem, even though the steak lives up to its billing. But the undeniable magnificence of the meat affirms a suspicion that creeps into all arguments about steak: good breeding does make a difference. —*H.T.*

NEW YORK STRIP STEAK WITH SERRANO LIME BUTTER

Lonesome Dove Western Bistro, Fort Worth

Serves 4

4 (14-ounce) dry-aged Prime New York strip steaks
1/2 cup peanut oil
Coarse salt
Cracked black pepper

Serrano Lime Butter
1/2 pound unsalted butter
2 Serrano chilies, roasted
3 cloves garlic, roasted
3 limes, juiced
2 tablespoons salt

TIP
Grass-fed steak requires 30% LESS cooking time. Be careful not to overcook.

Brush oil on steaks that have been allowed to warm to room temperature, and season liberally with salt and pepper. For medium-rare steaks (between ½ to 2 inches thick), sear for 1 1/2 minutes on each side on a 400 degree grill, then roast on the cooler side of the grill. Remove from heat and let rest for 10 minutes. Warm before serving and plate with Serrano Lime Butter.

To make the Serrano Lime Butter, puree roasted chilies, garlic, and lime juice in a food processor.

In a mixer, whip the butter until soft. Add the chile mixture and salt and whip for 3 minutes.

RANCH-ROASTED PRIME RIB

Perini Ranch Steakhouse, Buffalo Gap

Serves 6 to 8

Prime rib roast (1 pound per person)
1 cup coarsely ground salt
2 cups coarsely ground black pepper
1/3 cup flour or cornstarch
1/3 cup garlic powder
1/3 cup dried oregano

Tom Perini developed a love for ranch life growing up and working on his family's ranch. In 1973 he turned that passion into a career, becoming America's popular cowboy gourmet. After perfecting the traditional cowboy cuisine and creating a few recipes of his own, Perini moved from the back of the chuckwagon into his own restaurant on the family's working ranch. Since 1983, Perini Ranch Steakhouse has served as home to some of the best chuckwagon-style food in America. The restaurant is located on the Perini Ranch in Buffalo Gap, Texas (population 463).

Combine all dry ingredients and rub on both sides of the meat to create a crust.

Preheat oven to 500 degrees.

Place the roast on a wire rack set into a roasting pan to keep it away from the drippings and roast for 25 minutes to seal the juices. Reduce the temperature to 300 degrees and roast to desired doneness, using a meat thermometer.

BUFFALO TENDERLOIN PEPPERSTEAK WITH SMOKED WHISKEY CREAM SAUCE

Bonnell's Fine Texas Cuisine, Fort Worth

Serves 1

1/4 teaspoon kosher salt
1 teaspoon cracked black pepper
1 (8- to 9-ounce) buffalo filet
1 teaspoon canola oil
1 tablespoon butter
1 clove garlic, minced
1 small shallot, finely chopped
2 tablespoons, plus 1 ½ teaspoons
  McKendrick's Mesquite-Aged Whiskey
  (Jack Daniel's plus 1 drop liquid smoke
  may be substituted)
1/4 cup heavy cream

Mix the salt and pepper together and spread evenly onto a large plate. Press the filet down into the seasoning to coat thoroughly on both flat sides.

In a medium-size skillet on high heat, brown the steak on both sides in canola oil. Place the pan and steak in a 350 degree oven and finish cooking until desired temperature is reached.

Remove steak from pan and allow to rest while making the sauce.

To make the sauce, use the same pan, and add the butter, shallot, and garlic. Sauté until lightly brown and then add the whiskey. Be careful to do this away from the flame because the whiskey will flame. If using an electric range, light match and stand back. After whiskey has burned out, add the cream and reduce to a slightly thick consistency that will coat the steak. Pour the sauce directly over the cooked filet, allowing the sauce to run down all sides, and serve hot.

Serve with your favorite side dishes.

Bonnell's Fine Texas Cuisine is currently rated one of the Top 3 Restaurants in the Dallas/Fort Worth Metroplex by the Zagat *Survey of Texas Restaurants and has won the Award of Excellence from* Wine Spectator *in 2004, 2005, 2005, 2006, 2007 and 2008. The food is pure Texan, with a modern twist.*

Jon Bonnell, Bonnell's Fine Texas Cuisine

TEXAS TWO-STEP: CALF FRIES AND BLADE STEAKS

Riscky's Steakhouse, Fort Worth

Serves 2

In 1911 Polish immigrant Joe Riscky came to Fort Worth and went to work at Armour Packing Company in the stockyards for $9 a week. He and his wife, Mary Bunkervitch, opened Riscky's Grocery & Market in 1927, where they began offering lunches featuring their homemade barbeque. The menu has since expanded and—although not for the squeamish—the award-winning calf fries are a must.

Calf Fries
1 pound calf fries (beef testicles, each the size of a medium egg or smaller)
1 1/2 pint whole milk
2 whole eggs
4 ounces flour
4 ounces corn flour
1 tablespoon corn starch
1 tablespoon black pepper
3/4 tablespoon salt

1/2 teaspoon baking soda
1/4 teaspoon onion-garlic powder
Oil for cooking

Blade Steaks
4 (6-ounce) blade steaks
Salt
Pepper
Garlic, crushed

Heat 2 inches of oil to 375 degrees.

To prepare the calf fries, thaw, if frozen, until they are icy but not fully thawed. The membrane (tissue covering the organ meat) must be removed before cooking. In order to do so, cut the fry in half and push the membrane against the meat in an effort to turn the fry inside out. Take a paring knife and gently separate the two. Cut the fry in half again, quartering.

Create an egg wash by combining milk and eggs together in a small bowl. In a medium bowl, mix all other ingredients except the calf fries.

Place calf fries in egg wash and then in bread mixture, patting the flour into the meat to avoid moist spots. Repeat process once more, generously forcing more breading onto the meat.

Place the breaded meat into the hot oil for 3 to 5 minutes, or until they float.

Season the blade steaks with salt, pepper, and garlic to taste. Grill the steaks over mesquite chips to desired temperature. Serve with a side of calf fries and your favorite vegetable.

PORTERHOUSE STEAKS WITH WILDCATTER STEAK RUB

Wildcatter Ranch Steakhouse, Graham

Serves 4 to 6

1 to 1 1/2 cups Wildcatter Steak Rub *(recipe follows)*
4 porterhouse steaks, about 1 inch thick
3 teaspoons olive oil

To prepare the steaks for grilling, place the rub on a wide plate. Rub each steak with oil and place steak on top of the rub. Pat ample amounts of rub onto both sides of steak. Place on a grill over medium heat, coals will be ashy. Grill for 14 to16 minutes for medium-rare (145 degrees internal temperature) to medium (160 degrees internal temperature), turning once.

Transfer steaks from the grill to a platter and allow the steaks to rest for 5 minutes. Remove the steak from the bones and carve into slices.

Steak Rub
(makes approximately 2 cups)
1/3 cup beef base, or stock
1 tablespoon kosher salt
1/2 cup coarse black pepper
1 tablespoon cornstarch
2 tablespoons oregano
1/2 cup paprika
1 tablespoon dry thyme leaves
1 teaspoon onion powder
1 teaspoon cinnamon
1 teaspoon granulated garlic
1 tablespoon minced garlic

Mix together in a small bowl and reserve, or cover and refrigerate for future use.

A wildcatter is someone who drills wells in the hope of finding oil in territory not known to be an oil field. In the early 1920s, those were the individuals who frequented this area of Texas.

As the oil fields were developed, short-lived boom-towns emerged, some within sight of this very restaurant. Seated atop a bluff overlooking some of the most beautiful land in Texas, a visitor can gaze across the Palo Pinto Hills, enjoy the best food in Texas, and imagine the colorful past of Wildcatter Ranch.

The menu is true Texan featuring hand-cut, mesquite-grilled steaks.

Wildcatter Ranch

CORNMEAL AND RED CHILE-CRUSTED BEEF TENDERLOIN

Backstage Steakhouse and Garden Bar, Spicewood

Serves 6

16 tortillas, softened
4 cups white cheddar
1 1/2 pounds fresh baby spinach, washed
6 (6-ounce) beef tenderloins
1 cup cornmeal
1/4 cup New Mexico Red Chile Flakes
1/4 cup plus 2 tablespoons flour
Salt to taste
2 eggs
3 to 4 tablespoons heavy cream
3 tablespoons butter
Chicken stock
Ancho Chile Butter *(recipe follows)*
Tomatillo Sauce *(recipe follows)*

Ancho Chile Butter
Oil for frying
1 stick butter
1 teaspoon chili powder
1 ancho chile
1 shallot, finely diced

Tomatillo Sauce
1 1/4 to 1 1/2 pounds tomatillos
1 fresh jalapeño, or 2 Serrano peppers, stemmed, and seeded
1 1/2 to 2 cups chicken stock
1 cup onion, diced
1/2 cup cilantro, chopped

To wilt the spinach, heat a large skillet to medium-low heat, add 2 tablespoons olive oil or butter and add the spinach in 3 or 4 batches. Keep turning until all spinach has been added. Drain off liquid and let cool.

Preheat oven to 350 degrees. Soften tortillas in hot oil for 2 to 3 seconds. Grease an 8 x 8-inch baking dish and line with 4 softened tortillas. Add 1/3 of the spinach, 1/4 of the cheese and 3/4 cup of tomatillo sauce. Repeat layering until spinach is used and end with cheese and sauce as the top layer. Place in the oven for 15 to 20 minutes, or until cheese is lightly browned. Allow to cool, and cut into 12 equal portions.

Beat eggs and cream to make the egg wash. By pounding, flatten tenderloin to ½ inch thick and season with salt and pepper. Dip one side in egg wash and press into cornmeal and red chile mixture.

Cook chile-side down in medium hot skillet for 2 to 3 minutes, then flip and cook for another 4 to 5 minutes for a medium-rare steak.

To prepare sauce, stir butter and 2 tablespoons flour together in a pan over medium heat for 2 to 3 minutes. Add chicken stock and stir to make a veloute (a white sauce made with stock). Transfer the warm veloute to a small pan and gradually whisk in chile butter until incorporated.

To make the Ancho Chile Butter, remove the seeds from the ancho chile, discard seeds, and fry chile for 20 to 30 seconds in oil no hotter than 275 degrees. Drain and let cool. Using a coffee grinder or food processor, grind chile into medium-sized flakes. Using a hand or standing mixer, add butter, shallots, chile powder, and chile flakes, and mix on high speed until well blended. May be stored in a separate container.

To make the Tomatillo Sauce, combine all the ingredients in a large saucepan and bring to a boil. Turn heat to medium-low and simmer for 15 to 20 minutes or until vegetables are tender. Add mixture to blender, and using a low puree setting, slowly pulse until blended.

Serve steak with Smashed Potatoes *(see recipe, p. 139)* and pour sauce around the plate.

Chef Raymond Tatum is a native Austinite, who has showcased his talents in some of Austin's finest restaurants for more than 22 years. At Jeffrey's, Raymond earned the Texas Monthly "Star" rating, and maintained that rating during his 12-year association with them. He was voted Best Chef in Austin in 1995 by the Austin Chronicle's *Reader's Poll. Raymond has also been featured on the PBS series "Great Chefs of the West."*

BASEBALL CUT TOP SIRLOIN PRIME STEAK

Star Cafe, Fort Worth

Serves 8

1 (11-ounce) Prime top sirloin steak,
  cut to resemble a baseball
Coarse black pepper
Garlic salt

Lemon Butter Sauce
1 tablespoon butter, softened
1 teaspoon lemon juice

The oldest restaurant in the Historic Fort Worth Stockyards, this cafe works hard at maintaining its Old West flavor. Don't pass up this top sirloin steak—it's a home run every time.

Sprinkle the steak with black pepper and garlic salt. If cooking on a flat grill, season it with the lemon butter sauce to flavor the steak and keep it from sticking to the flat surface. If cooking on a charcoal grill, sprinkle the lemon butter sauce onto the steak. This will cause the fire to flame up over the steak, forming a light crust around the meat.

To make the Lemon Butter Sauce, whip the lemon juice into softened butter.

CHAMPIONSHIP PRIME RIBEYE STEAK WITH POMEGRANATE CRÈME SAUCE

Canary by Gorji, Addison

Serves 4

4 (14-ounce) Prime ribeye steaks
1 tablespoon olive oil
Kosher salt
Coarse ground black pepper
Pomegranate Crème Sauce *(recipe follows)*

Pomegranate Crème Sauce
1 tablespoon olive oil
1 teaspoon butter
2 ounces sliced mushrooms
1 ounce julienned red onions
Kosher salt
Coarse ground black pepper
4 ounces heavy cream
1 tablespoon pomegranate puree
1/4 teaspoon Sumac *(found in specialty grocery stores)*

This restaurant, Canary by Gorgi, may seem an odd choice for a steakhouse cookbook, considering it's a New Mediterranean restaurant. Notwithstanding that fact,, Chef Gorgi is a two-time winner of the annual Texas Steak Cookoff and Beef Symposium in Hico, Texas. This is his award-winning recipe.

Let steak sit at room temperature for 15 minutes.

Combine salt, pepper, and olive oil. Brush both sides of steak with mixture and let sit 5 more minutes.

Grill steak on high flame, 2 1/2 minutes per inch, on each side for medium rare. Be careful to turn the steak only once. While cooking, prepare Pomegranate Crème Sauce.

To make the Pomegranate Crème Sauce, heat olive oil and butter on high and sauté the mushrooms, red onions, salt, and pepper until the red onion starts to lose its color.

Add the cream and pomegranate puree and mix. Simmer for 2 minutes, but do not boil.

Drizzle on steak or serve on the side. Garnish with fresh pomegranates.

CHICKEN FRIED STEAK

Line Camp Steakhouse, Tolar

Serves 10 to 12

10 to 12 (6-ounce) top round steaks,
   pounded and tenderized
4 eggs, beaten
5 cups flour
1/2 cup black pepper
1/4 cup salt
1/2 cup garlic powder
1/2 cup onion powder
Extra virgin olive oil

Put beaten eggs in a shallow bowl. In a separate bowl, mix together all dry ingredients. Dip steak into eggs, then into flour mixture.

Heat extra virgin olive oil to cover the bottom of pan or skillet. When skillet is hot, add the steak. Brown one side, then flip to brown the other. Serve with cream gravy *(see p. 83)*.

CRUSTED TENDERLOIN BEEF TIPS

Lisa West's Double Nickel Steakhouse, Lubbock

Serves 4

2 tablespoons butter
1 tablespoon chopped garlic
1 large shallot
1 teaspoon fresh thyme, finely chopped
3/4 cup beef broth
1/2 cup Burgundy red wine
16 ounces beef tenderloin
1/8 cup coarse salt
1/8 cup coarse ground black pepper
Flour, enough to coat
2 tablespoons clarified butter

Advertising themselves as "a young restaurant with an old soul," Lisa West's Double Nickel Steakhouse is located in the panhandle of West Texas—the heart of cotton, cattle, and oil country, where the people know their steaks.

Since opening the Double Nickel in 2005, owner Lisa West has seen her establishment mentioned on many "best of" restaurant lists.

Melt 1 tablespoon butter in a heavy skillet over medium-high heat. Add garlic, shallot, and thyme. Sauté until shallot is tender, about 5 minutes. Add broth and wine. Boil until sauce is reduced to ½ cup, about 12 minutes. Set sauce aside.

Cut beef into 3/4-inch cubes. Combine salt, flour, and pepper and toss beef tips in the mixture.

Heat clarified butter in a medium skillet over medium-high heat. When butter is hot, add coated beef tips to skillet and cook to desired doneness, about 5 minutes for medium-rare. Transfer crusted beef tips to 4 warm plates. Reserve skillet.

Pour sauce into reserved skillet. Bring to a boil, stirring to scrape up browned bits. Boil 2 minutes. Whisk in remaining tablespoon butter. Salt and pepper to taste.

Spoon sauce over beef tips and serve hot.

FOIE GRAS FILET MIGNON WITH WILD MUSHROOMS

Bailey's Prime Plus, Fort Worth

Serves 4

4 cups seasonal wild mushrooms
2 tablespoons butter
2 tablespoons white truffle oil
1/2 cup demi-glaze concentrate, *(available
   at most groceries)*
1/4 cup red wine
1/4 cup heavy cream
Salt and pepper to taste
4 (2-ounce) portions foie gras
4 (10-ounce) portions filet mignon
Italian parsley, for garnish
French sea salt

Sauté mushrooms in butter and truffle oil in a saucepan over medium heat until golden brown and lightly crispy. Deglaze pan with red wine and add demi-glaze. Stirring with a wooden spoon, slowly drizzle heavy cream into pan, being careful not to break up mushrooms. Remove from heat and let rest at room temperature.

Season filet mignon liberally with salt and pepper and grill to desired temperature. Let rest for at least 5 minutes.

Just before serving, score an "X" pattern onto the portions of foie gras using a paring knife. Lightly season with salt and pepper and sear quickly on high heat on both sides until soft to the touch and just turning golden brown. Remove from heat.

To serve, place sautéed mushrooms in center of plate, place the filet on top and the foie gras in the center of the filet. Garnish with fresh chopped Italian parsley and a French sea salt.

Bailey's Prime Plus is a new upscale steakhouse crafted by prominent Dallas restaurateur Ed Bailey.

Bailey believes that a well-crafted menu, a dedicated staff to deliver impeccable service, an award-winning wine list and an over-the-top atmosphere with comfortable elegance are what make a steakhouse truly great.

AGING—WET VS. DRY

There are two kinds of aging today—wet and dry. Dry aging is both how it used to be done and how it still tends to be done in fancy-shmancy steakhouses and high-tone markets. The process is time-consuming and expensive, and was the way all beef was treated through the 1960s and '70s. These days 90% of all beef is wet-aged. It's easy and cheap—and for the home cook, the beauty of the process is that it can happen in their own refrigerator. Big producers of steak rely on slaughterhouses, wholesalers or supermarkets to wet-age for them.

The starting point for either wet or dry aging is the same: a slab of fresh beef. Oddly, fresh beef isn't all that alluring; in fact, it's tough as an old shoe and in desperate need of something to soften it up. If beef is left all by itself for a few days, its own enzymes go to work breaking down fibrous connective tissue and muscle and it self-tenderizes. It's always nice when a product does the work itself, and both the wet- and dry-aging processes use this capacity to their advantage.

Here's how wet-aging works: a beef carcass is cut up and slabs or individual steaks are vacuum-sealed in plastic. Moisture loss is minimal and taste isn't compromised. The meat is refrigerated for at least a week while it languishes in its own juice (that's why it's called "wet"). Self-tenderizing automatically stops after about 11 days, but the beef can be kept for up to four weeks under refrigeration before it's sold. Most producers will sell their product after about a week.

Dry-aging takes more time and costs more money, so it's no surprise that it has more cachet. You'll hear steak enthusiasts speak of "dry-aging" in reverent tones although it's not a glamorous process. Basically, slabs of un-wrapped beef are placed on open shelving or hung up in a meat locker where the air is kept moving around it. It's cold in there (around 33 degrees) and the humidity is low (50%). As the meat tenderizes it is also losing moisture, thus intensifying the flavor.

The caveat is that meat that's dry-aged must be carefully monitored for bacteria growth—and that especially goes for anyone trying this at home. It's alright if the meat grows a little mold, or even if it develops a crust—you can trim that off. But it's imperative that you keep the temperature close to freezing in order to fend off pesky bacteria.

Dry-aging can take anywhere from two to eight weeks. Longer than that and you've got a mushy steak, but somewhere in between is the time when the steak develops those luscious characteristics you hear referred to as "buttery" and "nutty". And that's when connoisseurs get light-headed. They'll pay a lot for this sensation, and a tell-tale sign that they're enjoying the experience is that they're eating their steak unadorned. They've paid a lot for that steak and they want to taste every penny's worth.

—H.T.

SEARED TENDERLOIN WITH CHIMICHURRI AND TOASTED GOAT CHEESE

Del Frisco's Double Eagle Steak House, Dallas and Fort Worth

Serves 6

6 (8 to 10-ounce) filet mignon steaks
    (ideally, USDA Choice, center cut), 3 inch cut
12 ounces goat cheese (Chevre)
2 cups prepared Chimichurri Sauce, room
    temperature
Salt and pepper to taste
Olive oil

Chimichurri Sauce
1 cup chopped fresh parsley (no stems)
2 teaspoons fresh garlic, chopped
3 teaspoons fresh oregano, chopped
1/2 cup olive oil
2 teaspoons red wine vinegar
1 teaspoon kosher salt
1 teaspoon black pepper
1 teaspoon crushed red pepper

This fabulously beautiful steakouse looks like a modern version of an upscale, turn-of-the-century fine dining establishment.

Del Frisco's has made a name for itself with great steaks and a wagonful of dining awards, including: the 2008 AOL Top Steakhouse Dallas award; the 2006 Dirona Award Winner; Ivy Award Recipient; Member of the Fine Dining Hall of Fame; Wine Spectator's Award of Excellence; Open Table's Top Booked Steakhouse in Dallas; Zagat-Top Rated in Dallas; D Magazine's Top Steakhouse; and a place on the Texas Monthly Top Steakhouses in Texas list, 2007.

Preheat oven to broil setting.

Coat cast iron skillet with olive oil and wipe dry. Place on medium-high heat. When skillet first begins to smoke, place generously seasoned filet mignon steaks on skillet and sear one side for 4 minutes without moving. Turn steaks over and sear other side for 3 minutes.

After searing steaks set aside for 15 minutes to rest. After rested, crumble goat cheese on top of steaks, place on sheet pan and place under broiler. Leave until steaks are heated and goat cheese has lightly browned.

As steaks are heating, prepare the Chimichurri Sauce. Combine all ingredients in a medium bowl. Cimichurri should be served at room temperature.

Remove steaks from oven and ladle 2 to 3 ounces of prepared Chimichurri Sauce over each steak and serve.

STEAK AU POIVRE

Lisa West's Double Nickel Steakhouse, Lubbock

Serves 2

2 (8-ounce) boneless strip steaks,
    1/2 -inch thick
1 tablespoon whole black pepper,
    crushed with a rolling pin
1 tablespoon unsalted butter
4 tablespoons Worcestershire sauce
1/2 tablespoon A-1 sauce
1 tablespoon cognac
4 tablespoons heavy cream
1 tablespoon chopped parsley
2 tablespoons chopped chives
1 teaspoon lemon juice

Press pepper into steak. Let stand 20 minutes.

Trim the fat from the beef and sauté in a heavy iron skillet. When the fat begins to melt, remove it from the pan and place steaks in pan. Cook on high flame until well browned on one side, then turn over. For medium or well-done steak, reduce heat. When steak is cooked to desired temperature, remove from skillet and let stand on dinner plate for a few minutes.

To make the sauce, remove grease from skillet. Return skillet to fire and add butter, heavy cream, Worcestershire sauce, A-1 sauce, parsley, chives, lemon juice, and cognac. Stirring, reduce sauce until it thickens, then pour over steaks and serve.

"The best way to have a quiche for dinner is to make it up and put it in the oven to bake at 325 degrees. Meanwhile, get out a large T-bone, grill it, and when it's done, eat it. As for the quiche, continue to let it bake, but otherwise ignore it."

—Texas Bix Bender,
author and humorist

24-OUNCE BONE-IN RIBEYE

Al Biernat's Restaurant, Dallas

Serves 1

1 (24-ounce) aged ribeye
Kosher salt
Black pepper
Herbs de Provence

With thirty years of experience as a restaurateur, Al Biernat has worked his way up to join the ranks of the elite steakhouses.

Beginning his career in the industry as a bartender at the Paragon in Aspen, Colorado, Biernat got a taste of the satisfaction that comes with pleasing high-profile customers that expect great food and want to be entertained as well. With his charming personality, Biernat is a fixture at his popular restaurant, which opened in June 1998.

Wet the steak and season with kosher salt and black pepper. Sprinkle meat with mixture of herbs de Provence (marjoram, thyme, savory, basil, rosemary, sage, lavender). Let meat sit with seasoning for 5 minutes. Grill over medium-high heat approximately 7 to 10 minutes per side for medium rare. Cooking time may vary depending on the heat of the grill.

TIP
Take the steak out of the refrigerator and let it rest 15 minutes before you put it on the grill.

FLAME ROASTED NEW YORK STRIP WITH SHINER BOCK DEMI-GLAZE AND DRUNKEN ONIONS

J.R.'s Steakhouse, Colleyville

Serves 2

2 (16-ounce) New York Strip
  steaks, Prime or Choice, cleaned
  and cut
1 dash kosher salt
1 dash pepper, freshly cracked
2 tablespoons butter, melted

Demi-Glaze
2 cups Shiner Bock Beer
4 ounces sweet Texas onion,
  finely diced
1 ounce Worcestershire sauce
2 tablespoons brown sugar
2 ounces heavy cream
4 ounces beef demi-glaze

Drunken Onions
2 sweet Texas onions, cut into
  thickly sliced rounds
1 dash salt and pepper
3 ounces Shiner Bock Beer
1 tablespoon butter, melted

Preheat grill and clean the grates.

In a small saucepot, combine the beer, diced onion, Worcestershire sauce, brown sugar, heavy cream, and the beef demi-glaze.

Heat the mixture on the stove over medium-high heat. Bring to a slow boil and allow it to reduce until the mixture thickens to a sauce consistency. Strain sauce and keep warm.

To make the Drunken Onions, season the onions with salt and pepper. Place on grill and baste with butter. Cook until tender. Place onions in a bowl and allow to marinate in the beer.

Season the New York strips with salt and pepper. Place on a clean, hot grill and baste with butter. Cook until desired doneness is achieved. Serve steak over the demi-glaze and top with Drunken Onions.

GRILLED MUSHROOM FILET

J.R.'s Steakhouse, Colleyville

Serves 2

3 tablespoons olive oil
2 (10-ounce) beef tenderloins, center cut
Pepper, fresh cracked, to taste
Salt to taste
1 ounce butter, melted
6 ounces veal demi-glaze *(recipe follows)*
3 ounces butter, cubed and cold
6 ounces mushrooms, wild blend
2 ounces brandy

Veal Demi-Glaze
5 pounds veal bones
5 cloves garlic, whole
2 quarts chicken broth
1 ounce fresh thyme

8 peppercorns
4 bay leaves
1 ounce fresh basil
4 tablespoons tomato paste
1 pound (2 medium-size)
  onions, chopped
1/2 pound carrots, chopped
1/2 pound celery, chopped
2 cups red wine
1 pint fresh blackberries
1 pint fresh blueberries
1 pint fresh strawberries,
  chopped
2 ounces honey

Chef Todd Phillips presides over this casually elegant steakhouse just west of the DFW airport, serving up steaks, seafood and specialty dishes. The atmosphere is serene, with a fireplace, stone walls, subdued lighting and white tablecloth presentation.

Preheat grill to high. Slightly rub filets with 2 tablespoons olive oil. Heavily season the outside of the filets with the cracked pepper and salt. Gently place the seasoned filets on hot grill. Cook on each side until desired temperature is reached. Place cubed butter on top of filet and allow to rest for at least 5 minutes.

Heat a heavy gauge sauté pan on stovetop over medium-high heat. Add a drizzle of olive oil when pan is hot. Add mushrooms and butter, and roast mushrooms until they brown. Deglaze pan using the brandy. Add veal demi-glaze and bring sauce to a simmer. When ready to serve, pour sauce over each filet.

To make the demi-glaze, preheat oven to 375 degrees. Place bones in roasting pan. Roast bones in oven until golden brown, about 3 hours. Remove from oven and place bones into a stockpot. Discard grease from roasting pan and deglaze with red wine. Scrape bottom of pan to get all the drippings. Add drippings and all remaining ingredients to stockpot and cover with water. Place stockpot on stove over medium-high heat. Cook for 6 to 8 hours at a low simmer. Drain off stock into another stockpot. Place on stove over high heat. Reduce by half. Place finished sauce into a food storage container and reserve, or refrigerate until needed.

VICKI'S CHICKEN FRIED STEAK WITH FIRE ROASTED GREEN CHILIES

Youngblood's Stockyard Cafe, Amarillo

Serves 8

8 steaks, half frozen (preferably a lean piece
   of pectoral meat, or the trimmings from a top sirloin)
Hobart Meat Tenderizer
3 eggs
1 pint buttermilk
Flour
Salt
Pepper
Clarified butter or margarine
8 green chilies

Tenderize your steaks using Hobart Meat Tenderizer or another meat tenderizer. Preheat a griddle or large skillet on medium heat.

Roast chilies over an open burner on the stovetop until dark brown or almost black. Once roasted, place chilies in a baggy or paper bag and let stand for several minutes. Remove from bag, and peel, seed, and chop.

Make an egg wash by combining buttermilk and eggs in a bowl. In a low bowl or plate, season flour with salt and pepper to taste. One at a time, place steaks in wash and then dredge in flour. Shake off extra flour and place on a parchment paper-lined pan or cookie sheet.

When all steaks are breaded, heat a half stick of butter in the hot skillet. Cook steaks on both sides until golden brown and the middle of the steak is done.

To serve, place steaks on warm plate, cover with country gravy and top with fire-roasted green chilies.

Praise in a review from the New York Times*: "Youngblood's Stockyard Cafe is the real deal: Diners just don't get any more cowboy than this. Tucked away at the site of one of the largest livestock auctions in the world, this restaurant is smoky, old-fashioned, and furnished with cowhides, burlap, and the requisite taxidermy. But it's the food that keeps those cattlemen coming."*

You can't argue with the truth—just try this chicken fried steak and you'll agree.

BUCK REAMS' SOURDOUGH CHICKEN FRIED STEAK

Grady's Restaurant, Fort Worth

Serves 6

"Only a rank degenerate would drive 1,500 miles across Texas without eating a chicken fried steak."

—Larry McMurtry, *In a Narrow Grave: Essays on Texas*

Sourdough Starter
1 (1 1/4 -ounce) package active dry yeast
1 cup sugar
6 cups all-purpose flour
4 cups warm water

Chicken Fried Steak
1 tablespoon kosher salt
1 teaspoon freshly ground black pepper

2 cups all-purpose flour
1 teaspoon freshly ground white pepper
4 to 6 cups peanut oil, or enough to completely cover the steaks in a Dutch oven
6 tenderized beef steaks, pounded thin

To make the sourdough starter, fill a large crock or large bowl with the water. Sprinkle the yeast over the top and let it dissolve for at least 4 minutes. Using a long spoon or whisk, stir in the sugar and flour. Loosely cover with plastic wrap and set the mixture aside at room temperature for at least 12 hours before using. When ready to use, pour into a wide, shallow bowl.

Whisk 2 cups flour, salt, and both peppers together in a bowl. Place in a shallow dish or plate and set aside.

Pour the oil into a Dutch oven or a large, heavy, deep-sided skillet, and set the pan over a fire or on a stove over medium-high heat. Heat the oil to 375 degrees, using a thermometer to determine the temperature.

While the oil is heating, bread the steaks. One at a time, dip a steak into the flour, then into the sourdough starter, completely coating the steak. Finally dip it into the flour once again, completely coating it. Set the prepared meat on a wire rack over a clean sheet pan until there are enough steaks coated to fill the pan without crowding.

When the oil is ready, gently slide 2 or 3 steaks into the hot oil. Cook the steaks for 4 to 6 minutes, turning once, taking care not to break the coating. After the steaks are cooked, place them on a sheet pan lined with paper towels to drain. Repeat the cooking process, allowing the oil to again heat to 375 degrees before adding the next batch of steaks. Repeat the cooking process. Season with salt and pepper while the steaks are hot. Serve immediately with ketchup or gravy.

More
BEEF

In a perfect world, some of us would eat steak every day, but even in Texas it is acceptable to mix it up occasionally—with other beef dishes, of course.

Here are some recipes that will sate your appetite for everything beef. From ribs, sausage, and brisket, to salads, sliders, and burritos, these recipes will keep you and your beef buddies grill-happy for a long time.

No beef bible would be complete without a bow to Texas's official dish—chili. It would be easy to fill an entire cookbook with the many great Texas chili recipes, but with a great deal of hand-wringing and teeth- gnashing, we cleared the field for one award-winning recipe, Riscky's Brick Chili. It's the real thing.

BEEF RIBS

Smoke, at the Belmont Hotel, Dallas

Serves 8

Short ribs
1/3 cup chili powder
1/3 cup smoked paprika
2 tablespoons granulated garlic
1 tablespoon ground cumin
1 teaspoon finely ground cayenne pepper
1/2 cup kosher salt
2/3 cup dark brown sugar
3 tablespoons granulated sugar

A dry rub and curing is important with large or bone–in meat cuts, such as ribs or beef brisket. A dry rub is a mixture of seasoning: chili powder, ground spices, sugar, and salt. The rub will cure the outer portion of the meat with a heavy flavor, leaving the interior unseasoned. In the case of a long smoking time needed for a beef brisket or short ribs, a dry curing rub results in the charred outer "bark". There will be a pink smoke ring under the bark, achieved by low, slow, and totally dry cooking.

Combine chili powder, paprika, garlic, cumin and cayenne pepper in a small bowl and set aside.

Combine the sugars and salt in a food processor and pulse to combine. Add the spices one quarter at a time, pulsing the mixture after each addition. Slowly add in the coffee.

Apply 2 tablespoons rub mixture per pound of meat, rubbing generously onto the meat. Let meat marinate, covered, overnight in the refrigerator before grilling or smoking.

The standard cooking time for ribs is about an hour per pound, fat side up, under dry indirect smoke at a steady temperature of 190 degrees. Cook until the bone pulls easily from the meat.

The spice rub can be stored in a 1-quart mason jar. The spice rub will lose some of its aroma over time after long storage, but it can be lightly re-toasted in the oven if this happens.

BBQ BEEF BRISKET WITH CHILE RUB AND COFFEE CURE

Smoke, at the Belmont Hotel, Dallas

Serves 8

Beef brisket
1/3 cup chili powder
1/3 cup smoked paprika
2 tablespoons granulated garlic
1 tablespoon ground cumin
1 teaspoon finely ground cayenne pepper
1/2 cup kosher salt
2/3 cup dark brown sugar
3 tablespoons granulated sugar
1/3 cup finely ground dark roast coffee

In this newly renovated 1940s hotel, you can enjoy the farm-to-fork dining that Smoke restaurant offers under the creative direction of Chef Tim Byres.

Byres has created a unique dining experience—not an easy feat for food-savvy Dallasites—featuring hardwood-smoked, made-from-scratch sausage, ribs, and brisket, as well as jams, mustards, and sauces.

Combine chili powder, paprika, garlic, cumin and cayenne pepper in a small bowl and set aside.

Combine the sugars and salt in a food processor and pulse to combine. Add the spices one quarter at a time, pulsing the mixture after each addition. Slowly add in the coffee.

Apply 2 tablespoons rub mixture per pound of meat, rubbing generously onto the meat. Let meat marinate, covered, overnight in the refrigerator before grilling or smoking.

Note: The spice rub can be stored in a 1-quart mason jar. The spice rub will lose some of its aroma over time after long storage, but it can be lightly re-toasted in the oven if this happens.

The standard cooking time for brisket is about an hour per pound, fat side up, under dry indirect smoke at a steady temperature of 190 degrees.

Serve with pickled cabbage, pickle slices, or your side of choice.

RANCHMAN'S CHICKEN-FRIED STEAK FINGERS WITH CREAM GRAVY

Ranchman's Ponder Steakhouse, Ponder

Serves 6

6 (6-ounce, 1/2 -inch thick) slices
   of inside round steak
Course salt
1 egg
2 cups milk
2 cups flour
1 tablespoon salt
2 teaspoons black pepper

Ranchman's Cream Gravy
3/4 cups canola oil
1 cup all-purpose flour
1 teaspoon black pepper
1 teaspoon salt
1 quart whole milk
1 cup water

Using a sharp knife, trim the steak slices of any fat or gristle. Pound each piece with the coarse side of a tenderizing mallet until it is double in size and half as thick. Cut each piece into 6 strips.

In a bowl, make an egg wash by beating together the egg and milk, and set aside.

Make seasoned breading by mixing flour, salt, and ground black pepper, and reserve on a plate.

Preheat at least 1/2 inch of cooking oil in a deep skillet, or heat a deep fat fryer to 340 degrees.

Dredge the steak in the seasoned flour, dip it in the egg wash, then return it to the flour. Push the flour into the steak with your fingers to be sure that there are no moist spots. (The steak will spread out a little.) Immediately slide the steak fingers into the hot oil and fry on one side until golden and crispy, then turn and cook until done. The steaks are done when you lift them with a pair of tongs and the meat is stiff, not floppy. Serve with a bowl of gravy.

To make the Cream Gravy, begin by making a roux, combining canola oil and flour in a saucepan, and stirring constantly until the mixture is smooth. Cook, continuing to stir, until roux looks grainy and color changes slightly from white to barely golden. Remove from heat. Add black pepper and salt and mix well.

Add milk and water to the roux and cook over high heat. Beat with a wire whisk until well blended. Keep whisking until gravy comes to a boil and thickens. Add hot water to thin gravy, if needed. Remove from heat to prevent scorching. Gravy should be the consistency of pancake batter. The local term for gravy is "Cowboy Puddin." Save any leftover gravy—it will reheat well, but may need to be thinned with water when reheated.

Dave Ross owns and operates the Ranchman's Cafe—also known as Ranchman's Steakhouse—as well as the Old Lumberyard antique shop and a soap business in Ponder, Texas. Their soap is made from the fat captured in the restaurant and features special scents.

Ranchman's food has been featured in several magazines, including Gourmet, Southern Living, Texas Monthly *and two shows on the Food Network—FoodNation with Chef Bobby Flay and "The Best of" with Marc Silverstein.*

TENDERLOIN SALAD

Taste of Texas Restaurant, Houston

Serves 6

This recipe is multi-layered, but the effort and time involved is well worth it. The salad can easily serve as a main course for dinner—real steak goodness at a fraction of the cost.

In 2007, the AOL City's Best guide chose the Taste of Texas Restaurant for their coveted "City's Best Steakhouse" award.

Marinated Steak Skewers
2 pounds certified Angus beef
   tenderloin tails
1/2 cup soy sauce
1/2 cup Worcestershire sauce
1/2 cup sherry
3 tablespoons minced garlic
1 cup fresh pineapple juice
1/2 cup dark brown sugar

Sautéed Red Onions
1 medium red onion, thinly sliced
1 tablespoon unsalted butter
1 tablespoon olive oil
1 tablespoon Worcestershire sauce
1 teaspoon minced garlic

Candied Almonds
(makes 2 cups)
2 cups sliced almonds
6 tablespoons unsalted butter
1/2 cup sugar
1/2 teaspoon coarse kosher salt
1/4 teaspoon black pepper
1/4 teaspoon ancho chili powder
Pinch cayenne pepper

Fried Blue Cheese
4 ounces Maytag Blue Cheese,
   cut into 1-inch squares
1/2 cup all-purpose flour
1/2 teaspoon salt
1/2 teaspoon black pepper
1/4 teaspoon garlic powder
1/2 cup Panko
2 eggs, beaten
Oil for frying

Cilantro Vinaigrette
1 1/2 cups olive oil
1/2 cup white balsamic vinegar
3 cloves of minced garlic
2 1/2 fresh jalapeños, trimmed
   and seeded
2 1/2 limes, juiced
1 bunch cilantro, chopped
3 tablespoons honey
2 teaspoons sea salt

Salad
1 pound mixed greens
1 avocado, sliced
1 grapefruit, cut into sections

Mix all ingredients, except the tenderloin tails, together in a gallon ziplock bag and set aside. Cut the tenderloin tails into 1-inch pieces and thread 4 pieces onto each skewer. Gently place the skewers in the marinade bag, being careful not to tear it, and let marinate for at least 1 hour.

(Continued on p. 86)

Grill the skewers over medium-high heat, 2 minutes per side, or until meat is nicely seared. Transfer the skewers to the medium-low side of the grill, or turn the heat to low, and continue cooking to desired doneness.

In a skillet over medium-high heat, add the butter and olive oil. Once butter is melted, add garlic and sauté until it becomes aromatic. Add the onions and sauté until caramelized, about 3 to 5 minutes. Add the Worcestershire sauce and mix. Remove from heat and set aside.

To make the Candied Almonds, first preheat oven to 350 degrees.

In a saucepan, heat the butter and sugar, stirring occasionally, for 10 minutes. Add the salt, pepper, chili powder, and cayenne, and mix well. Pour the sugar mixture over the almonds and mix well. Spread almonds in a thin layer onto a cookie sheet, and bake until well browned, stirring several times.

To make the Fried Blue Cheese, beat eggs in a medium-size bowl. In a separate bowl, mix the flour, Panko, salt, pepper, and garlic powder. Dip the squares of blue cheese into the egg mixture, then the flour mixture, and repeat this batter process twice.

In a medium skillet, heat 1 inch oil to 275 degrees. Fry battered cheese until golden brown. Drain on a paper towel.

To make the Cilantro Vinaigrette, blend the garlic, jalapeño, lime juice, cilantro, honey, and sea salt together. Add the balsamic vinegar and mix well. Add the oil slowly, mix well, and set aside or refrigerate before serving.

To assemble the salad, toss mixed greens together with 1 cup of the cilantro vinaigrette. Place mixed greens onto 4 serving dishes or plates. Top each with sautéed red onions, candied almonds, grapefruit and avocado slices. Pull the tenderloin off the skewers and place 4 pieces on top of each salad. Place 1 square grilled cheese on top of each salad and serve immediately.

Taste of Texas Restaurant

ONION JAM AND TEXAS GOAT CHEESE SLIDERS

Grady's Restaurant, Fort Worth

Makes 12 sliders

2 1/2 pounds ground chuck
3/4 cup goat cheese
2 tablespoons kosher salt
1 tablespoon coarse ground
   black pepper
12 fresh biscuits, or mini hamburger
   buns
12 slices cheddar cheese (optional)

Onion Jam
(makes 2 cups)
1 large yellow onion, julienned
1 large red onion, julienned
2 bunches green onion, chopped
2 tablespoons oil
3/4 cup balsamic vinegar
1/2 cup brown sugar

Sliders are little hamburgers that, if done right like these, carry a big punch. Don't be fooled by the small amount of beef in each, they are juicy and filling and are sure to inspire eating contests with your friends—if you make enough and want to share!

The jam is a brilliant spicy-sweet addition. If you like onions, you'll find other uses for this wonderful jam.

Prepare a grill to medium-high heat.

To make the onion jam, heat the oil in a large skillet over medium heat. Add the onions, sautéing them until they start to soften. Stir in the vinegar and brown sugar, reduce the heat to simmer, and cook until the vinegar has been reduced by half. Remove and cool.

In a large mixing bowl, combine the ground chuck, goat cheese, onion jam, salt, and pepper. Blend thoroughly, using your hands. Divide the mixed ground chuck into 12 patties making sure they are compacted and firm.

Place the patties on the grill and cook for 7 to 8 minutes on each side or until done. Before the meat is finished, place 1 slice cheddar cheese on each patty. Serve with the onion jam on the side.

BURRITO DE PICADILLO

H&H Car Wash and Coffee Shop, El Paso

Serves 4 to 6

1 teaspoon tomato boullion with chicken flavoring
1 teaspoon pepper
1 teaspoon garlic power
1 teaspoon onion powder
1/4 teaspoon ground cumin
1 1/2 pounds (100% lean) ground beef
4 to 6 jalapeños, chopped
2 to 3 tomatoes, chopped
1/2 white onion, chopped
1/2 pound Muenster cheese, coarsely grated
8 to 10 flour tortillas

This wouldn't be a Texas beef book if it didn't give a nod to the Mexican beef dishes that abound. This odd combination of car wash and cafe is no secret to Texas foodies— I've been told by some of the best in the business that H&H is possibly the top restaurant in Texas. Taste their burritos and you will be a believer as well.

Frommers says, "A dinky coffee shop straight out of the 1960s, the H&H is a bit weathered, noisy, and not much to look at. It doesn't matter—the place is home to some of the best inexpensive Tex-Mex in town."

In a small bowl, mix tomato boullion, pepper, garlic powder, onion powder, and cumin. Sprinkle it on ground beef and thoroughly mix.

Brown the ground beef in a large skillet over medium heat. When the ground beef is almost cooked through add the jalapeños, tomatoes, and onion. Turn heat to low, cover, and let simmer for about 10 minutes.

When picadillo meat is done, warm the tortillas (either in the microwave for a few seconds on high, or in a warm oven). Spoon the picadillo meat onto the middle of the tortilla, sprinkle with Muenster cheese, roll up and enjoy.

CARNE PICADA BURRITO

H&H Car Wash and Coffee Shop, El Paso

Serves 4 to 6

1 teaspoon tomato boullion with
  chicken flavoring
1 teaspoon pepper
1 teaspoon garlic power
1 teaspoon onion powder
1/4 teaspoon ground cumin
1 1/2 pounds tri-tip chuck roast, trimmed
  and cut into bite-sized pieces
4 to 6 jalapeños, chopped
2 to 3 tomatoes, chopped
1/2 white onion, chopped
8 to 10 flour tortillas

Mix tomato boullion, pepper, garlic powder, onion powder, and cumin together. Set aside.

Make sure the chuck roast is cut into bite-sized pieces and trimmed of all fat.

In a large skillet, brown the chuck roast pieces in a little oil. When the beef is almost cooked through, add the jalapeños, tomatoes and onion. Cover and let simmer for about 10 minutes on low heat.

When meat is done, stir in the spice mixture.

Warm the tortillas, spoon the meat onto the middle of the tortilla, roll up, and enjoy.

RISCKY'S BRISKET STEW

Riscky's Steakhouse, Fort Worth

Serves 6 to 8

1 1/2 gallons water
2 pounds potatoes, peeled and diced
4 pounds potatoes, peeled and cubed
2 pounds peeled carrots, cut into 2-inch pieces
1 pound onions, peeled and cut into quarters
1 pound celery, cut into 2-inch pieces
1 bay leaf
3 cans whole peeled tomatoes, with liquid
4 tablespoons salt
2 tablespoons pepper
1 teaspoon granulated garlic
1 (3-pound) pre-cooked, oak-smoked brisket,
   cut into 2-inch cubes

TIP
*Freeze this stew
and save it for a
cold winter day.*

Pour water into large stock pot and add 2 pounds diced potatoes. Boil until potatoes are cooked to a mush, creating a thick, starchy water.

Add all vegetables, including the cubed potatoes, and spices to water in pot; cover, and cook over high heat until the stew comes to a boil. Turn heat down and simmer until vegetables become tender, about 45 minutes. Add brisket to pot and continue to simmer 10 to 15 minutes.

Remove from heat and serve with cornbread.

CHILI CULTURE

It's impossible to write a book about Texas beef recipes without a respectful bow to the deceptively humble bowl of chili. Entire books have been written about this popular dish; contests held and prizes given for the best recipes; arguments won and lost about the proper ingredients (Texans do NOT put beans in their bowls). So much has been written about chili that we've put the facts into a basic overview for you.

★ Chili con carne is the Spanish name for a stew that is made with "peppers and meat".

★ American pioneers and trailhands used a combination of dried chile peppers, beef, suet and salt, pounding the mixture into bricks which could be boiled to make chili along the journey.

★ There are many tall tales about cowboys, but the International Chili Society tells this one and it has the ring of historical truth. There was once a range cook who made chili along all the great cattle trails of Texas. He collected wild oregano there, chile peppers, wild garlic, and onions and mixed it all with the fresh-killed beef or buffalo (whatever he had at hand) and the cowhands loved it. To ensure he had an ample supply of native spices wherever he went, he planted gardens along the paths of the cattle drives—mostly in patches of mesquite—to protect them from the hooves of the cattle. The next time the drive went by that spot, he found his garden and harvested the crop, hanging the peppers and onions and oregano to dry on the side of the chuckwagon.

Another undocumented piece of history goes like this: Frank and Jesse James ate a few bowls of "red" before pulling many of their bank jobs. At least one town was spared their mayhem by having a local chili parlor. Fort Worth had a chili joint just north of town, and the James boys rode in there just for the chili, vowing never to rob their bank because "any place that has a chili joint like this just oughta be treated better."

★ An old black range cook once prayed this chili prayer. His name was Bones Hook, and the prayer went:

Lord, God, you know us old cowhands is forgetful. Sometimes, I can't even recollect what happened yesterday. We is forgetful. We just know daylight from dark, summer, fall, winter, and spring. But I sure hope we don't never forget to thank you before we eat a mess of good chili.

We don't know why, in your wisdom, you been so doggone good to us. The heathen Chinese don't have no chili, never. The Frenchmen is left out. The Russians don't know no more about chili than a hog knows about a sidesaddle. Even the Mexicans don't get a good whiff of chili unless they live around here.

Chili-eaters is some of your chosen people, Lord. We don't know why you're so doggone good to us. But, Lord God, don't never think we ain't grateful for this chili we are about to eat. Amen.

★ Pat Garrett is supposed to have said of William Bonney— aka Billy the Kid: "Anybody that eats chili can't be all bad."

★ For more than 100 years, Hispanic women would bring cauldrons of chili con carne to Military Plaza in downtown

San Antonio, build fires to reheat their spicy stew, and sell it by the bowl to passersby. These women were called the "chili queens" of San Antonio. The stands were finally shut down in the 1940s, but San Antonians' love for chili remained.

★ At the 1893 Columbian Exposition in Chicago, the "San Antonio Chili Stand" introduced chili con carne to America and it quickly gained national popularity (so, yes, chili is a Texas creation).

★ Prior to World War II, hundreds of small, family-run chili parlors (also known as "chili joints") had popped up throughout Texas and other states, particularly those where Texans had moved to make new homes. Each claimed to have their own secret recipe.

★ Chili con carne became the official dish of the state of Texas in 1977, according to the House Concurrent Resolution Number 18 of the 65th Texas legislature.

★ Wick Fowler, north Texas newspaperman and inventor of Two-Alarm Chili, added tomato sauce to his chili — one 15-ounce can for every three pounds of meat. He also believed that chili should never be eaten immediately, but refrigerated overnight to blend the flavors properly. He made a Texas-size fortune marketing a chili "kit" complete with spices. His Two-Alarm Chili is famous for its punch. If you couldn't take the heat, Fowler's chili instruction advised this: For 1-Alarm Chili, use only half of the red pepper. For False-Alarm Chili, leave out the red pepper. For 3-Alarm Chili or hotter, merely add hot peppers. Matt Weinstock, a Los Angeles newspaper columnist, once remarked that Fowler's chili "was reputed to open eighteen sinus cavities unknown to the medical profession."

★ Texas boasts scores of qualifying chili cookoffs that lead up to the big one in Terlingua, Texas. More than thirty preliminary competitions are listed on the Original Terlingua International Championship Chili Cookoff site. One of the more famous of these qualifying contests is the Chilympiad—a Texas tradition since 1970, and held annually the second week of September. It is billed as the olympics of chili cooking. Originally the cookoff was held in San Marcos, Texas, at Aquarena Springs, but in 1974 the event established permanent headquarters at the Hays County Civic Center in San Marcos. Winners of this contest automatically qualify for the world championship cookoff in Terlingua, Texas.

The rules are few and simple: First, all chili must be made from scratch onsite at the contest; and second, women are barred from entering the contest as chefs. In response to this somewhat arbitrary rule, another cookoff was established in Luckenbach, Texas, named "Hell Hath No Fury Like A Woman Scorned," in which the winners similarly qualify for Terlingua's world championship cookoff, establishing a sort of equal opportunity chili heat.

★ Frank Tolbert, who owned a chain of chili parlors in Dallas, founded the Terlingua International Chili Championship. For the last 66 years, on the first weekend of November, thousands of "chiliheads" convene in Terlingua for what has become the Original Terlingua International Frank X. Tolbert – Wick Fowler Championship Chili Cookoff—the most famous chili cookoff in the world.

Three days of events include an Ugly Hat contest, a Golf Shoot-Out, lots of boot-kickin' music, the World Championship Margarita Mix-Off, and chili cookoff. In the late 1970s the chili cookoff sponsored a "Mexican Fence-Climbing Contest" to spoof the U.S. Government's planned reinforcement of the chain-link fence separating El Paso, Texas from Cuidad Juárez, Mexico. The fence the "chiliheads" built was constructed by undocumented Mexican workers. Just goes to show, times change—chili doesn't.   —J.S.

RISCKY'S BRICK CHILI

Riscky's Steakhouse, Fort Worth

Serves 8 to 10

10 pounds coarse ground chuck
1 pint water
4 ounces granulated garlic
5 ounces flour, sifted
5 ounces chili powder, sifted
1 stick margarine, melted
Choice of accompaniments

Mix water, salt, garlic, and margarine together and pour in skillet. Heat until boiling, then add half the ground chuck. Stir meat until browning begins, pushing it around the skillet. Do not be too aggressive with the stirring spoon—you do not want to break up the meat overly much—keep it a coarse grind. When the meat begins to brown, add the remaining 5 pounds chuck and continue to push meat around the skillet.

In a small bowl, combine the flour and chili powder.

Before meat is fully cooked, add the flour and chili powder mixture to meat. Blend thoroughly and let simmer for 10 minutes.

Serve the chili hot with grated cheese, purple or white onion, jalapeño peppers, and your choice of corn chips, crackers, cornbread, cooked macaroni pasta, or sour cream. Chili can be stored in a container and frozen for future use.

This Riscky's Steakhouse is smack in the center of the Historic Fort Worth Stockyards, and is on every "best of" steak list. The chili, however, is made in bricks at their other Fort Worth location, Riscky's BBQ, which used to be a grocery store. The chili bricks, smoked ribs, and a few other menu items are shared with their sister restaurant.

FACT
Chili is the official dish of the state of Texas

Riscky's BBQ-Deli

SWEET PAPRIKA AND FENNEL SEED SMOKED SAUSAGES

Smoke, at the Belmont Hotel, Dallas

Makes 5 pounds

3 pounds beef chuck, lean
1 1/2 pounds pork butt, ground
1 cup BBQ Beef Chili Rub *(see recipe, p. 161)*
1/2 cup smoked paprika
2 tablespoons kosher salt
1 cup non-fat dry milk
1/3 cup whole toasted fennel seeds
Natural pork casing

Grind meat to a medium grind. Combine ground meat, Chili Rub, paprika, kosher salt, and dry milk and re-grind. Fold in the fennel seeds, being careful not to break the seeds.

Refrigerate 2 hours, then stuff into 1-pound links.

To smoke in a multiple-shelf, indirect heat-sourced smoker, remove bottom and middle racks and replace with sausage dowels. Preheat pit and smoke sausages on bottom rack at 130 degrees for 45 minutes, or until the skin is dry. Raise the sausage dowels up a shelf to 165 degrees and smoke until internal temperature reaches 150 degrees. Remove sausages to an ice bath to halt cooking. Refrigerate for at least one day to let meat set.

The Belmont Hotel's restaurant pays homage to the old fashioned smokehouse tradition, and serves up some of the tastiest sausages and ribs in the Lone Star state.

Sausages are not difficult to make and the difference in taste is well worth the effort. Once you've mastered the technique, you'll want to experiment with spices to make your own favorite recipe.

Beef Jerky: A Serious History

To say that beef jerky is a delicacy is stretching the analogy a bit for those who only know the dry, tasteless, chemically altered, molar-cracking version found at many truckstops along America's highways. Sure, we all ate it when we were kids. Once they were old enough to shed their baby teeth but too young to drink, it became a test of manhood for young boys in my Texas hometown to swear they liked, no, loved beef jerky.

The real beef jerky— the Indian/pioneer/cowboy favorite that sustained generations through lean times when fresh game wasn't available —is something that has engendered a fanatic following among Texans and those outsiders lucky enough to find the real thing today.

Jerky is probably one of the oldest forms of portable food. Cut the meat of deer, buffalo, or other game into thin strips, remove the fat, salt it, and hang in the sun to dry for 2 or 3 days, and—voila!—you have a protein food that needs no refrigeration, no eating utensils, and can be easily transported. The word "jerky" comes from the South American Quechua Indian term charqui, which means "to burn," and much of our Texan tradition of jerky comes from the Indians.

In time, American pioneers figured out they could smoke the meat on a scaffolding over an open fire for a half day and get the same result. A good chuckwagon chef would not be caught dead without a supply of jerky for his men. It was inevitable that beef, in its relative abundance in Texas, would eventually become the most popular form of jerky.

Ask any truck driver where the best beef jerky can be found, and he will send you to the place that offers the good stuff, the homemade versions, the sweet and spicy flavor choices. Happy is the hungry traveler that stumbles upon the real thing.

For those seeking jerky enlightenment, all roads lead to Centerville, Texas. Billing itself as the Jerky Capitol of the World, Woody's Smokehouse is the main stop in Centerville—a veritable superstore of jerky delicacies, offering such tasty treats as smoked hickory peppered beef, teriyaki beef, jalapeño beef, mesquite beef and sweet an' spicy beef jerky.

If you have a secret hankering for jerky, but are afraid to come right out and admit it, listen up: beef jerky is a 97% fat-free bundle of protein (no empty calories there!) and is a healthier snack food than you can find in most peoples' grocery carts. So go ahead and hold your head up high, cowboys!   —J.S.

Found: The Missing Links
The Best Beef Sausage in Texas

....

Prasek's Hillje Smokehouse, El Campo

Maeker's, Shiner

Poffenberger's, Bellville

Louie Mueller Barbecue, Taylor

Guy's Meat Market, Houston *(hot links)*

Kreuz Market, Lockhart *(BBQ links)*

Meyer's, Elgin

Woody's Smokehouse, Centerville *(beef jerky)*

New Braunfels Smokehouse, New Braunfels

—J.S.

BEEF TENDERLOIN WELLINGTON

Bohanan's Prime Steaks & Seafood, San Antonio

Serves 8 to 10

1 (5 to 7-pound) Prime beef tenderloin, cleaned and trimmed
1 pound grade A foie gras
2 pounds roasted mushroom duxelles *(recipe follows)*
8 to 10 sprigs fresh thyme
3 to 4 sheets puff pastry, enough to totally encase the tenderloin
4 eggs, beaten
Salt and freshly cracked black pepper to taste
Marinade of your choice, enough to cover the tenderloin (optional)
4 cups Hollandaise, or Béarnaise sauce

Duxelles
5 pounds mushrooms (crimini, oyster, or chanterelle)
1/2 cup extra virgin olive oil
2 cups merlot
10 sprigs thyme, picked and finely chopped
8 shallots, finely chopped
Kosher salt
Freshly ground black pepper, to taste

Preheat oven to 350 degrees.

To make the Duxelles, mix the mushrooms with the 1/4 cup olive oil, salt, and pepper in a large bowl and toss to coat. Roast on a cookie sheet or roasting tray for 20 minutes, or until mushrooms are dark brown and the juices coming off have begun to dry in the pan. Remove the pan from the oven and allow mushrooms to cool.

In a large heavy-gauge pan, heat the remaining 1/4 cup olive oil. Add the shallots, and sauté until translucent, cooking over a low heat. As the shallots cook, chop the roasted mushrooms to a very fine consistency.

Add the chopped mushrooms to the shallots and cook over medium heat until remaining moisture evaporates. Deglaze the mushroom pan with the merlot then add the wine mixture to the mushroom pan. Add the chopped thyme and cook until all remaining liquid is absorbed. Remove the mushroom duxelles from heat and spread onto a pan to cool.

While the duxelles is being prepared, marinate the tenderloin, if desired, for 30 minutes.

Heat a large griddle on medium-high heat. Remove tenderloin from the marinade and season it with salt and pepper. Rub the griddle with a little bit of olive oil, then sear the tenderloin on all sides just until a nice crust has formed, about 1 minute each side. Remove from the griddle and place on a platter. Refrigerate immediately to stop further cooking.

When the mushroom duxelles is thoroughly cooled, begin to assemble the Wellington.

Roll the sheets of puff pastry lightly, using a floured rolling pin and board. Overlap the edges and use enough pressure to form a good seal.

When the pastry is rolled out, spread the duxelles in a thick yet even layer over the entire surface, leaving a 2-inch edge overlapping all sides. Cut the foie gras into 1/2-inch thick slices and place them in a row in the middle of the duxelles.

Place the chilled tenderloin on top of the foie gras, folding in the tail of the tenderloin to ensure proper cooking. Brush the edges of the puff pastry with the beaten eggs. Fold one edge of the pastry over the tenderloin, tucking the ends in. Roll the tenderloin to complete the Wellington. Brush the entire surface of the finished Wellington with the egg wash. Sprinkle with salt and pepper and arrange thyme sprigs on top in an eye-appealing manner. Brush again lightly with egg wash.

Coat a large roasting sheet with cooking spray or clarified butter. Transfer the Wellington roll to the sheet and cook the roll in a preheated 400 degree oven for 30 minutes, or until the pastry is golden brown. The meat will be medium rare. Additional cooking time may be needed if a more finished degree of doneness is desired.

Remove from the oven, carefully using spatulas, and transfer to a carving board. Allow the Wellington to rest 5 minutes. Using an electric knife, slice into 2-inch thick portions. Serve and top with desired sauce, either Hollandaise or Béarnaise.

Chef / owner Mark Bohanan realized his life-long dream in downtown San Antonio, Texas—Bohanan's Prime Steaks & Seafood. He has been recognized as one of San Antonio, Texas' finest Executive Chefs, and an up and comer in the culinary world. He is a member of the Chaine des Rotisseurs, the Texas Restaurant Association, and the Culinary Federation of America.

In 2007, Bohanan's was voted the #2 Best Steakhouse in Texas by Texas Monthly *magazine.*

TENDERLOIN TAMALES WITH PECAN MASH AND SUN-DRIED TOMATO CREAM

Reata Restaurant, Fort Worth

Makes 15 to 20

Since opening in 1995 as an unexpectedly good place to get a decent dinner in the small West Texas town of Alpine, Reata has expanded from the original tiny cottage to three off-site restaurants, including this landmark multi-story restaurant in downtown Fort Worth.

Masa Filling
2 1/2 cups masa
3 cups fresh corn (about 6 ears, off the cob)
1 1/4 cups lard, or vegetable shortening
1 cup Rich Chicken Broth *(see recipe p. 159)*
1 bunch cilantro, coarsely chopped
1 tablespoon kosher salt
1 tablespoon paprika

Tenderloin Filling
2 pounds ground tenderloin, or ground beef with at least 20% fat
1 yellow onion, finely chopped
1 red bell pepper, finely chopped
5 jalapeño peppers, seeded and diced
4 garlic cloves, minced
2 tablespoons ground cumin
2 tablespoons kosher salt
1 tablespoon ground coriander

Tamales
45 dried corn husks
1 to 2 gallons hot water

Pecan Mash
(makes about 1 1/2 cups)
3/4 cup pecan pieces
2 garlic cloves, coarsely chopped
1 bunch cilantro, finely chopped
3/4 cup Asiago cheese, grated
1 to 2 jalapeño peppers, seeded and diced
1 to 1 1/2 cups extra virgin olive oil
Kosher salt

Sun-Dried Tomato Cream
(makes about 5 cups)
1 tablespoon oil
2 garlic cloves, minced
4 tablespoons unsalted butter
1/2 cup rehydrated sun-dried tomatoes, pureed, or finely chopped
1 quart heavy cream
1/2 cup Parmesan cheese, grated
Kosher salt to taste
Freshly ground black pepper

To make the Masa Filling, combine all ingredients in a large mixing bowl. Using an electric mixer, process until well blended. The masa mixture should be the consistency of wet mud. To test, drop a spoonful of the mixture into a glass of cold water; if it floats, you have just the right amount of lard. If it sinks, add a little more lard, 1 tablespoon at a time, mixing well after each addition. Reserve.

To make the Tenderloin Filling, combine all the ingredients in a large bowl and mix well. Cover and refrigerate.

To make the tamales, soak 45 dried corn husks in hot water until pliable, usually about 1 to 2 hours. On a clean, dry work surface, place 2 corn husks end-to-end with about a 2-inch overlap in the middle. Grease your fingers well with lard or butter. Place 2 tablespoons of the masa filling in the center of each husk, spreading the filling to within 2 inches of the edges of the husks. Next, place a generous portion—about 3 tablespoons per tamale—of the tenderloin filling in the center of the masa. Tightly roll the husks up lengthwise around the filling, then fold or tie each end closed.

You can use some of the extra soaked husks and cut them into 1/8-inch-width strips to use for ties. You'll need 2 ties per tamale, one for each end.

Place half tamales in a single layer on a steam rack in a large pot filled with 1 1/2 inches of water, making certain the water does not touch the tamales. Cover with a tight-fitting lid. Cook tamales in 2 batches on high heat, covered, and steam for about 1 hour, adding water as needed to maintain the 1 1/2 inches of liquid.

Remove from pot and slice an opening in the top of each tamale. To serve, place the tamales on a platter and top with about 1 tablespoon of the Pecan Mash and at least 1 tablespoon of the Sun-Dried Tomato Cream.

To make the Pecan Mash, combine the pecans, garlic, cilantro, cheese, jalapeños, and 1/4 cup of the olive oil in a food processor. Pulse repeatedly to coarsely chop the pecans. With the machine running, slowly add the remaining olive oil, and process until all the oil is thoroughly incorporated. Season with salt. Cover and refrigerate.

To make the Sun-Dried Tomato Cream, heat the oil in a saucepan over medium-high heat. Add the garlic and sauté for about 2 minutes, until the garlic begins to brown. Add the butter and sun-dried tomatoes and cook for 1 to 2 minutes, stirring constantly. Lower the heat and slowly add the cream. Simmer for another 15 to 20 minutes, stirring constantly, until the liquid has been reduced by about half. Add the cheese and stir well. Season with salt and pepper. Remove from the heat and serve warm, or refrigerate until you're ready to reheat for future use.

LOVE BURGER

Love Shack, Fort Worth

Serves 4

4 ground brisket and tenderloin patties
4 slices American cheese
4 hamburger buns (recommend
   Mrs. Baird's 4-inch buns)
16 slices Love Shack (or your choice) pickles
4 slices large red tomatoes
1 ounce shredded Iceberg lettuce
2 ounces Love Sauce (available online)

Cook patties over a hot grill until desired temperature is reached. Assemble meat, cheese, pickles, tomatoes, and lettuce and add Love Sauce.

When is a burger not just a burger? When it's a Love Burger! Chef Tim Love serves possibly the most famous burger in the country out of his Historic Stockyards outdoor burger joint. Daily and nightly you can scarf down versions of this burger—I like the one served with the quail egg—and dance till the cows come home.

STARTERS, SIDES, SAUCES & RUBS

Cowboys need their vegetables, too, and these traditional side dishes are chuckwagon-worthy and downright scrumptious.

Over the centuries, the presentation has changed, but the star players are still the same: potatoes, corn, tomatoes, cheese, onion rings, hominy, grits, and beans.

And don't overlook the rub recipes that are featured at the end of this chapter, on pages 160-161. Getting a chef's secret rub recipe is a bit difficult, to say the least—these recipes are guarded like gold—but we have some great ones to share. Just keep 'em to yourself, okay?

GUY LEE'S PAN DEL CAMPO WITH CHEESE AND GREENS

Grady's Restaurant, Fort Worth

Serves 8

1 pound (about 20 slices) bacon
1 can (8 count) refrigerated biscuits
1/2 cup all-purpose flour, sifted
1 cup cilantro-nut mash
4 ripe Roma tomatoes, sliced into
    thin rounds
3 cups grated Monterey Jack cheese
1 1/2 cups goat cheese
2 cups field greens, washed and
    patted dry

Cilantro-Nut Mash
(makes 1 cup)
1 cup fresh cilantro, chopped
¼ cup grated Parmesan cheese
½ cup chopped pecans
2 cloves garlic, minced
¼ cup olive oil
2 tablespoons goat cheese
Kosher salt

Preheat the oven to 375 degrees.

In a heavy skillet, cook the bacon until very crisp (fry in batches if necessary to prevent over-crowding). Drain on paper towels, crumble, and set aside.

Remove the biscuit dough from the can and cut or pull apart into 8 equal pieces. Sprinkle some flour on a clean, dry work surface, flour a rolling pin, and roll each of the dough pieces out to approximately 9-inch rounds; don't worry about making them too thin, because the thinner they are, the crisper, lighter, and better they'll taste. Carefully transfer them to baking sheets and bake for 10 minutes or until browned. Remove from oven. Increase the oven temperature to 400 degrees. Spread each crust with some of the Cilantro-Nut Mash and cover evenly with crumbled bacon, tomatoes, and cheeses.

To make the Cilantro-Nut Mash, combine the cilantro, cheese, pecans, and garlic in a food processor. Pulse gradually, adding the oil. Add the goat cheese and season with salt, processing just until slightly smooth.

Return to the oven for 2 to 3 minutes or until the cheese has melted. Remove and garnish with the field greens. Serve immediately.

FACT
Pan del campo, meaning "camp bread," was recently designated the "official bread of Texas."

JALAPEÑO-CILANTRO SOUP

Reata Restaurant, Fort Worth

Serves 6

1/2 tablespoon unsalted butter
5 jalapeño peppers, seeded
    and minced
2 tablespoons garlic, minced
3/4 cup red onion, finely chopped
1 avocado, peeled and diced

4 Roma tomatoes, diced
8 cups heavy cream (use the
    highest fat content available)
Kosher salt
Freshly ground black pepper
1 bunch cilantro, stemmed and
    chopped

This fiery soup will warm your cockles (and everything else!) in any season. You can adjust the heat by adding or subtracting the number of peppers.

In a large stockpot, heat the butter over medium heat. Sauté the jalapeños, onions, and garlic for about 10 minutes, or until the onions are translucent and the peppers turn soft.

Remove from the heat and add the avocado, tomatoes, and cream. Lower the heat, then return the pot to heat, stirring constantly so the cream doesn't separate. Slowly bring the soup back to a simmer, cooking until liquid is reduced by 1/3. Stir often to prevent scorching or sticking.

Season with salt and pepper. Just before serving, add the cilantro, reserving about 1 teaspoon per serving for garnish. Sprinkle with the reserved chopped cilantro and tortilla crisps.

STUFFED MUSHROOMS

Line Camp Steakhouse, Tolar

Serves 8 to 10

A long-time steakhouse favorite, stuffed mushrooms are made more elegant with this cream cheese version.

48 to 60 medium mushrooms, stems removed
1 1/2 pounds cream cheese
1 1/2 teaspoons garlic
3/4 teaspoon salt
3/4 teaspoon pepper
1/2 cup grated Parmesan cheese (plus a
    little more for topping)
1/2 cup fresh chopped chives
1/2 cup chopped almonds
Garlic butter

Preheat the oven to 375 degrees.

In a medium bowl, mix together cream cheese, garlic, salt, pepper, Parmesan cheese, chives, and almonds by hand or using a mixer. Fill mushroom caps with mixture.

Put garlic butter and stuffed mushrooms in a 13 x 9-inch baking pan and sprinkle with Parmesan cheese.

Bake for 8 to 12 minutes, or until golden in color.

ROASTED TOMATO AND JALAPEÑO SOUP WITH LIME CRÈME FRAICHE

Bonnell's Fine Texas Cuisine, Fort Worth

Serves 4 to 6

3 to 4 fresh jalapeños
15 ripe Roma tomatoes
1 extra large sweet onion, sliced
   into 1/4-inch rings
3 to 4 cloves garlic, chopped
1 1/2 tablespoons extra virgin olive oil
1 1/2 cups water
2 limes, juiced
1 1/4 teaspoon kosher salt
1/2 teaspoon Bonnell's Creole
   Seasoning Blend *(recipe follows)*
Pepper to taste
2 to 3 tablespoons sour cream,
   for garnish

Creole Seasoning Blend
10 tablespoons iodized salt
4 tablespoons granulated garlic
4 tablespoons fine black pepper
1 tablespoon cayenne
1 1/2 tablespoons thyme, fried
   in a little oil
1 1/2 tablespoons dried oregano
5 3/4 tablespoons paprika
2 tablespoons onion powder
1 tablespoon dried basil

Slice the jalapeños in half, cut off the stems, and remove half of the white veins and seeds.

Grill the jalapeños, tomatoes, and onions until well charred on the outside.

In a large soup pot, lightly simmer the onions, tomatoes, jalapeños, and garlic with olive oil and water for 1 to 2 hours.

To make the Creole Seasoning, toss all ingredients together in a bowl and store in an airtight container.

When soup is ready, puree with a stick blender, strain, add lime juice, and season with salt, seasoning, and pepper. Optional garnish: top with a little lime-flavored sour cream and chopped cilantro, or jalapeño slices.

How many ways can I say I love tomato soup? Start with this one. It has a definite lean toward Mexican cuisine, which is the first thing I love about it. And the taste treats just keep on coming: lime, jalapeño, sour cream, and cilantro—yum!

NINE MILES OF DIRT ROAD

Hunter Brothers' H3 Ranch, Fort Worth

Serves 2

5 ounces refried beans
2 ounces guacamole
2 ounces sour cream
1/2 teaspoon taco seasoning
2 ounces pico de gallo *(recipe follows)*
1 1/2 ounces black olives
1/2 ounce shredded cheddar
1/8 ounce diced green onion

Pico de Gallo
1 tomato, finely chopped
1/2 onion, diced
1 jalapeño, seeded and diced
Handful cilantro, finely chopped

To make the Pico de Gallo, thoroughly mix all ingredients.

In the bottom of a small, round 6-inch iron skillet, spread beans, guacamole, and sour cream. Evenly sprinkle taco seasoning over sour cream. Top with pico de gallo, black olives, cheese, and green onions. Bake in a 350 degree oven until cheese just starts to melt, about 5 to 7 minutes. Serve with warm tortilla chips. You can double or triple this recipe.

In the 1800s, three brothers emigrated to the U.S. from Scotland with their parents. The brothers—William, Robert and David Hunter— enjoyed the opportunities and excitement presented to them in America's Old West. The name "H3" stands for the three Hunter brothers, who founded H3 Ranch in Nebraska.

Descendants of the Hunter brothers created this restaurant in the stockyards. Their dishes are creatively named for cowboy terms and phrases that date back to the cattle driving days of that century.

Cattlemen's Steak House

Eric Sawyer, Hunter Brothers' H3 Ranch

WIFE OF KIT CARSON SOUP

Hunter Brothers' H3 Ranch, Fort Worth

Serves 8

3 pounds chopped, cooked
   chargrilled chicken
1/2 pound (1 stick) butter
1/2 pound chopped green bell pepper
4 pounds chopped yellow onion
2 pounds diced Poblano chilies
1 bunch cilantro, chopped
9 ounces tomato juice
20 tomatoes, diced, with juice
3 gallons of water
1 pound chicken base
6 1/2 ounces white vinegar
1 1/2 ounces fresh lime juice
4 ounces tomato paste
1 ounce chopped garlic
1 package corn tortillas

Heat butter and sauté peppers and onion in large stockpot until the onions are translucent. Add the garlic and cilantro and sauté for 2 minutes. Add the tomato juice, diced tomatoes, vinegar, lime juice and the tomato paste. Bring to rolling boil. Add chicken, remove from heat, garnish with fried tortilla strips and serve.

To fry the tortilla strips, cut corn tortills into 1/4-inch wide strips, and fry in at least 1 inch hot peanut oil, for 1 minute. Remove with a spatula and drain on paper towels.

Chef Brian Kirby of H3 Ranch snuck this Texanified version of chicken soup into the book, even though it's a steak cookbook. It was just too good not to use, and who could resist a recipe from the wife of Kit Carson?

ONION RINGS

Killen's Steakhouse, Pearland

Serves 2 to 4

2 onions, thickly sliced
2 cups flour
1 quart buttermilk
Salt and pepper to taste

These are killer onion rings. Use the sweeter onions that are available in your grocery for an added taste treat.

Put flour and buttermilk each in a separate bowl.

Peel onions, cut in half, and slice into rings. Separate the rings and dredge them in flour, then coat in buttermilk. Dredge again in flour, salt and pepper them, then fry rings in hot oil until golden brown. Transfer to paper towels to drain and serve hot.

. . . .

TEXAS AU GRATIN POTATOES

Taste of Texas Restaurant, Houston

Serves 8

3 Yukon Gold potatoes, peeled and
  sliced 1/8-inch thick
1 1/2 cups heavy cream
1 tablespoon fresh pressed garlic
3 tablespoons chopped green onions

1/3 cup grated Asiago cheese
1 teaspoon sea salt
1/4 teaspoon ground white pepper
1 cup Monterey Jack cheese,
  shredded

Mix all ingredients except the cheese and place mixture in a 13 x 9-inch baking dish. Top with the cup of Monterey Jack cheese. Cover with aluminum foil and bake at 300 degrees for 1 1/2 hours.

Remove the foil, and cook at 375 degrees for 5 minutes, or until top is brown.

After removing potatoes from the oven, allow them to rest for 10 minutes before serving.

BAKED BRIE

Taste of Texas Restaurant, Houston

Serves 8

1 small wheel Brie, rind scraped
3 sheets phyllo dough
4 tablespoons melted butter
4 tablespoons apricot preserves
1/2 cup toasted pecan pieces
2 tablespoons dark brown sugar

Always take a good look at what you're about to eat. It's not so important to know what it is, but it's critical to know what it was.

—Texas Bix Bender

Preheat oven to 350 degrees.

Split the wheel of Brie in half length-wise to make 2 wheels. Mix the apricot preserves with half of the pecan pieces (reserving the other half for the topping). Spread the apricot pecan mixture in between the two layers of Brie.

Lay the first sheet of phyllo dough on a dry surface and brush with melted butter. Lay the next sheet directly on top of the first layer and brush with butter again. Repeat with the third layer. Place the Brie wheel in the center of the phyllo and wrap to enclose the cheese. Trim away excess phyllo. Flip the Brie so that the smooth side is up, place on a cookie sheet, and top with dark brown sugar and remaining pecan pieces.

Bake for 15 minutes. Serve with grapes, apple slices, and your favorite crackers.

THE NEW FRONTIER

It turns out that the preferred setting in which you eat your steak depends a lot on whether you think of yourself as a city slicker or a cowpoke. The urban steakhouse might as well be on Mars if you are used to pulling your truck up to an old-time Texas steakhouse where some old gnarly guy is firing up your steak on a greasy grill. At an urban steakhouse, the atmosphere is masculine and clubby, the lighting is low, and the cook is a chef who has a name—and who's made a name for himself (sorry, ladies, but steakhouse kitchens are usually still a man's world). There are a couple of other differences: side dishes at these places are a big deal, in size as well as in concept. And you'll be presented with a wine list, so don't ask for a bottle of Shiner. The idea of the posh steakhouse has engendered an entire breed of chains, some quite respectable. They include Ruth's Chris Steak House in Austin, Dallas, Fort Worth, Houston, and San Antonio; Perry's Steakhouse in Austin, Katy, Dallas and San Antonio, Eddie V's Edgewater Grille in Austin; Fleming's Prime Steakhouse and Wine Bar in Austin; Pappas Bros. Steakhouse in Houston and Dallas; and Sullivan's of Austin. Clearly the idea of taking an American standby like the steak and making it great has challenged chefs to take ownership of the product and to cook up their own versions that are virtuosic and unforgettable.

At Bohanan's Prime Steaks & Seafood in San Antonio, you'll find chef and owner Mark Bohanan orchestrating the show, from cooking to decorating. Tables are dressed in white linen, the waiters wear suits and ties, and wine is presented at the table as if it's a rare prize (which, in some cases, it is). And Bohanan dares to go where other steakhouses fear to tread except when their customer calls ahead: he offers Akaushi steak on the menu every day. It's a pricey experience (around $100 for one of these finely marbled, ambrosial cuts) but guaranteed to change your life. There are also cutting edge appetizers like green figs stuffed with blue cheese, sided with Asian pear slices and candied jalapeño slices with whipped cream cheese, a recipe from Bohanan's mother. The talent runs in the family.

It's not unusual for the new breed of chef to have their own website and tv show in addition to their own restaurant. Grady Spears is one of the most charismatic. He's chef and owner of the eponymous Grady's in Fort Worth, host of "The Cowboy Kitchen," and cookbook author, but most of all he can take all the credit for what he likes to call Cowboy Cooking. In addition to maple-crusted tenderloin with deviled Hollandaise, Grady's is famous for quail tostadas; a spinach salad with candied bacon strips, sweet onions and blue cheese; and cream of tomato soup with sourdough croutons. The chef also offers cooking classes for those who want to know what it's like to be at home on Grady Spears' range.

There's a reason so many of the great steakhouses are in Fort Worth: The city is the site of the Stockyards, the historic center of the livestock industry in Texas. At The Lonesome Dove Western Bistro there, you are apt to find celebrity chef and owner Tim Love—an "Iron Chef" winner—meeting and greeting his clientele. It's surprising that he has time, considering that he's also got a saloon (The White Elephant), a hamburger joint (The Love Shack) as well as a trendy Euro-bistro, Duce nearby. Being a chef nowadays equals being an entrepreneur. Steak is a specialty at Duce, but there's also jazz and a contemporary menu that features items like hamachi with minced pear, serrano and fried garlic. Back at The Dove, you might want to try the lamb belly BLT with watercress and tomato slices while you read up on Love's latest adventures in *Food & Wine* magazine.

Also in Fort Worth, Jon Bonnell proves that nice guys don't have to finish last. The chef-owner of Bonnell's is beloved for his generosity as well as his menu. Bonnell used to be a teacher, and he still teaches, in a way. His luscious renditions of game—elk, venison, quail, and wild boar—make diners eager students of the Bonnell cooking style. It's inventive ("Oysters Texasfeller" has a Southwestern twang courtesy of a little cilantro) and makes his fans want to learn more from the master. Bonnell's been discovered: he's a regular on the Food Network and has been on Nightline and the Today show. Usually, though, he's either cooking at Bonnell's, out in the dining room greeting guests, or still teaching—students love his wine class at nearby Texas Christian University.

Tom Perini

No discussion of Texas steaks is complete without mentioning Tom Perini. The uber-chef owns and operates Perini Ranch Steakhouse in Buffalo Gap just outside Abilene. It's out in the sticks but somehow people have found it and come back for more. Perini is the master of open range cooking, and all meat here is cooked over a mesquite fire, then anointed with a dry rub that consists of garlic, salt, pepper, oregano and beef base. There are only three cuts offered: ribeyes, tenderloins, and strips. That's apparently not a drawback, since the place has been blessed with accolades for its great steaks by publications such as *Texas Monthly, Saveur, Gourmet,* and *The New York Times.* It's Perini's life, by the way, since the restaurant is on the family ranch which has been occupied by the family since the 1880s.

Lately, a new rage in steakhouses has proved hard to ignore—the Argentinian version of the American icon is, unbelievably, more over the top than our version is. Fogo de Chao opened in Dallas in 1996 boldly expecting to sweep their meat-loving neighbors to the north off their feet. In some ways, it has. American steakhouses offer the diner a single cut of meat in tandem with a couple of sides, but Fogo de Chao is a carnivore's Nirvana. Studly waiter-chefs garbed in gaucho outfits wind around the dining room endlessly, toting gargantuan platters stacked with meats (lamb, pork, chicken, beef, sausage, and more) sizzling on dagger-sized skewers. Diners pick and choose to their heart's content (well, maybe their hearts aren't that content) until they just can't eat another bite. It's culinary showmanship to the max and it never fails to thrill—or fill.

It wouldn't be a stretch to say that the new steak chef (or steakhouse if you're looking at places like Fogo de Chao as the pinnacle of exhibitionism) is into showmanship. But it's also a fact that the new breed of chefs is justifiably as proud of their menus as they are of themselves. They have become celebrities, and they've worked hard to achieve their celebrity. There's a big difference between being famous and just being a show-off, and in Texas, we know the difference.   —H.T.

BUTTER BEANS AND HAM SHANKS

Riscky's Steakhouse, Fort Worth

Serves 6 to 8

4 pounds ham shank
2 gallons water
2 pounds large dried lima beans

4 tablespoons salt
2 tablespoons pepper
1 teaspoon granulated sugar

Place ham in large stockpot and add water. Boil over high heat for 45 minutes to 1 hour until ham is tender. Remove ham and reserve the stock for the beans. Cube ham into large chunks and set aside.

Wash lima beans well and place in stockpot with ham stock. Boil beans for 2 1/2 hours, or until tender. Add the ham chunks and cook for another 10 minutes.

Portion beans into large serving bowls, making sure everyone gets some of the ham chunks. Serve with cornbread.

This dish is good anytime, but on a cold day, it is manna from Heaven. Also it's a good way to put that leftover ham shank to use.

BAKED POTATO SOUP

Taste of Texas Restaurant, Houston

Serves 8

2 russet potatoes
1 yellow onion, diced
1 teaspoon table salt
1 teaspoon white pepper
1 cup buttermilk
1/2 cup heavy cream

2 tablespoons unsalted butter
2 chicken bouillon cubes
1 cup water
Chopped crispy bacon, chopped
  chives, and grated cheddar
  cheese for garnish

Bake the potatoes, remove the skin, and cube. Place the butter and onions into a large pot and cook on low heat until they become soft and transparent. Do not burn the butter. Add the milk and cream. Bring to a boil. Add the chicken bouillon cubes, then the potato cubes, and stir until the soup thickens and the lumps are gone. Add water for consistency. Bring to a boil for about 15 minutes. Add salt and pepper. Top with bacon, chives and cheddar cheese.

FRIED SPINACH

Lonesome Dove Western Bistro, Fort Worth

Serves 2

1 quart peanut oil
1/4 pound fresh spinach, washed
Kosher salt to taste
Cracked black pepper to taste

The 2005 Zagat survey results recognize Lonesome Dove Western Bistro as having the best food in Fort Worth, winning the restaurant a spot in Zagat's coveted "America's Top Restaurants."

Heat peanut oil in a saucepan to 350 degrees.

Place spinach in a strainer, colander, or fry basket and set into hot oil. Note: as the spinach cooks it will pop loudly from the water that is in the greens.

Fry for about 30 seconds, remove, and place on paper towels to drain. Season with salt and pepper. Spinach should be crispy and very light. Serve immediately.

HORSERADISH MASHED POTATOES

Cattlemen's Steak House, Fort Worth

Serves 6 to 8

6 large potatoes, peeled and cut into wedges
1/2 cup butter, softened or melted
2 tablespoons of horseradish, or to taste
4 tablespoons sour cream
1 teaspoon salt
1/2 teaspoon pepper
1 cup warm milk

Boil potatoes until tender when pricked with a fork. Drain and mash with a fork in a large mixing bowl. Add butter, horseradish, sour cream, salt, and pepper. Using an electric mixer, slowly add milk until consistency is creamy and to your taste. Depending on the size of the potatoes, you may use more than 1 cup warm milk.

JESSICA'S FAVORITE GREEN CHILE HOMINY

Perini Ranch Steakhouse, Buffalo Gap

Serves 10 to 12

1 cup chopped onion, sautéed
5 (15-ounce) cans white hominy, drained and liquid reserved
1/2 cup hominy liquid
1 tablespoon juice of pickled jalapeños
1/2 pound cheddar cheese, grated
10 slices bacon, fried crisp and chopped, drippings reserved
1 cup green chilies, chopped
1 to 2 pickled jalapeños, seeded and chopped (optional)

Perini's food philosophy is simple: food should look good, taste good, and you should be able to recognize it! His signature Green Chile Hominy (made with bacon, cheddar cheese and green chilies) is a winner.

Sauté the onions in a little of the bacon drippings and put aside. Heat the hominy in a separate pan, stirring often. When heated thoroughly, add the hominy liquid and jalapeño juice, bring back to high temperature and add 3/4 of the cheese. When the cheese melts, add half the peppers and bacon and all the onion.

Pour into a 9 x13-inch baking pan and sprinkle with the remaining cheese, bacon and peppers. (At this point it can be refrigerated or even frozen, if you want to make it in advance.) Bake at 325 degrees until cheese on top melts, about 15 minutes (40 minutes, if refrigerated).

CREAMED SPINACH

Wildcatter Ranch Steakhouse, Graham

Serves 8

The Wildcatter Ranch Steakhouse is situated where pioneers and wildcatters created the history of Texas. A customer is directed to their wide porch to find a rocking chair and to "sit back, gaze across the Palo Pinto Hills, enjoy the best food in Texas and let your imagination take you back in time."

1 large yellow onion, chopped
1/2 cup (1 stick) plus 1 tablespoon unsalted butter
1/4 cup all-purpose flour
1 tablespoon salt
1 cup heavy cream
1/2 cup chicken broth
1 teaspoon ground nutmeg
1 teaspoon cayenne pepper
1 teaspoon garlic powder
5 strips bacon, cooked crisp and crumbled
4 ounces cream cheese
1/2 cup grated Parmesan cheese
1/4 cup slivered almonds, toasted
3 pounds spinach, washed, dried and coarsely chopped

In a small pan over medium heat, sauté the onion with 1 tablespoon butter until tender, about 5 to 10 minutes. Remove from heat and set aside.

In a larger pan, melt the remaining 1/2 cup butter and allow it to brown slightly. Over low heat, whisk in the flour, continuing to stir until the roux turns a light golden color. Add the cream, broth, nutmeg, cayenne, garlic powder, bacon, cream cheese, and Parmesan cheese. Mix all ingredients well and continue to cook over low heat until the cheese has melted. Add the sautéed onion, toasted almonds, and spinach, and mix well. Cook until thoroughly heated. Serve warm.

TEXAS CAVIAR

Big Texan Steak Ranch, Amarillo

Makes 5 cups

The Big Texan Steak Ranch has received many honors, top among them being included in Maxim *magazine's list of "Top 10 Steak Houses in America."*

2 (16-ounce) cans black-eyed peas, drained and rinsed
1 medium jalapeño, minced
1/4 small white onion, chopped
1/3 cup Italian dressing
1/2 green bell pepper, chopped
1 tablespoon season salt
2 tablespoons chili powder
2 tablespoons ground cumin
1/4 teaspoon ground red pepper

Combine black-eyed peas with all ingredients, and stir well. Refrigerate until well-chilled and serve with corn or tortilla chips. This dish is best when made the day before and allowed to chill overnight.

OFF-THE-COB CREAM CORN

Lisa West's Double Nickel Steakhouse, Lubbock

Serves 12

10 ears fresh corn, cooked and cut off the cob
1 cup heavy cream
1 cup milk
2 tablespoons sugar
1 teaspoon kosher salt
1/2 teaspoon white pepper
1/2 teaspoon black pepper
1/4 teaspoon Accent
1/2 teaspoon granulated garlic
1/2 teaspoon thyme
4 ounces (1/2 stick) salted butter
2 tablespoons flour

In a stockpot, combine the first 10 ingredients and slowly bring mixture to a boil. Reduce heat and allow to simmer for 3 minutes.

In a separate saucepan, bring the butter to a boil. Stir in the flour. Add butter and flour mixture to the simmering corn. Stirring occasionally, allow to simmer for 3 more minutes. Keep warm until serving.

SMASHED POTATOES

J.R.'s Steakhouse, Colleyville

Serves 2

1 tablespoon olive oil
12 ounces Red Bliss potatoes,
  cleaned and peeled
4 tablespoons butter, cubed
6 ounces heavy cream

1 stem fresh basil
4 ounces Boursin cheese
Fresh cracked pepper, to taste
Salt to taste

Place potatoes in heavy pot and cover with water. Place pot on stove, uncovered, over medium-high heat. Cook the potatoes until tender.

In a saucepan over low heat, mix the cream, butter, and basil while the potatoes are cooking. Drain potatoes and use a whisk to smash potatoes by hand. Add the Boursin cheese and the cream sauce and mix until the potatoes are smooth and creamy. Season with salt and pepper and serve immediately.

COWBOY POTATOES

Perini Ranch Steakhouse, Buffalo Gap

Serves 8 to 10

4 to 5 pounds new potatoes, cut into wedges
1 stick butter, melted
1 medium white onion, sliced
1 to 2 cloves garlic, finely minced
1 teaspoon salt
1 teaspoon ground black pepper
1/2 teaspoon ground dried oregano

Preheat oven to 350 degrees. Coat the potatoes in butter, toss with onion, garlic, and sprinkle generously with salt, pepper, and oregano. Place in a baking dish, cover with aluminum foil, and bake for 1 hour, stirring occasionally. After 1 hour, remove the foil and continue cooking for another 30 minutes.

ZUCCHINI PERINI

Perini Ranch Steakhouse, Buffalo Gap

Serves 10

1/2 pound ground beef
1/2 pound hot sausage
1 large onion, diced
Dash salt
Dash ground black pepper
1 (28-ounce) can whole tomatoes, mashed and drained
6 ounces tomato paste
1/4 cup tomato sauce
2 teaspoons oregano
Dash garlic powder
2 pounds zucchini, sliced 1/4-inch thick
1/4 cup freshly grated Parmesan cheese

Preheat oven to 350 degrees.

In an oven-safe pan, brown the ground beef, sausage, and onion. Add salt and pepper to taste. Add the whole tomatoes, tomato paste, and tomato sauce and stir. Add the oregano and garlic powder and simmer for 5 minutes. Add the zucchini. Mix thoroughly, then sprinkle with Parmesan.

Bake until cheese melts and starts to brown, about 10 minutes.

Tom Perini's unique approach to ranch-style cooking, coupled with his friendly Texas style, has gained him national and international recognition. Tom was named one of the "24 Reasons Why We Love Texas" by Saveur *magazine in 2009, and the destination steakhouse was listed by* Texas Monthly *as the third best steakhouse in Texas in 2007.*

Visitors to the ranch can relax outside under the stars, listen to the band, watch the kids chase the cats and dogs, and enjoy ranch living and Texas hospitality at its finest.

BLUE CHEESE AND BLUE CORN GRITS

Bonnell's Fine Texas Cuisine, Fort Worth

Serves 4 to 6

1 tablespoon butter
1 pint chicken stock
1 pint heavy cream
1 cup chopped sweet onion
3 to 4 cloves garlic, minced
4 ounces Brazos Valley blue cheese,
  cut into small pieces
8 ounces Homestead Gristmill blue corn grits
2 tablespoons Parmesan cheese, grated
1/2 teaspoon kosher salt

In a saucepan over medium heat, sauté the onions in butter and garlic until the onions become translucent and soft. Stir in the liquids and bring to a simmer.

Season with salt, then whisk in grits until fully incorporated. Simmer on low for 18 minutes, until the grits have soaked up the liquids and softened. Add in all of the cheeses and stir until they melt. Taste to correct seasoning and serve with just a crumble of blue cheese on top.

Note: If using instant grits, the cooking time will only be 5 minutes, but the stone ground grits are recommended because they are more flavorful.

LOBSTER CREAMED CORN

Bohanan's Prime Steaks & Seafood, San Antonio

Serves 10

12 ears yellow corn
1/4 pound unsalted butter
1/2 yellow onion, small dice
1/2 cup all-purpose flour
1/4 cup sugar
1 tablespoon Old Bay seasoning
1/4 teaspoon cayenne powder
2 cups heavy cream
1 pound Philadelphia cream
   cheese, room temperature

5 dashes Tabasco sauce
1 tablespoon lobster base
1/3 cup brandy
Salt and pepper to taste
10 (12-ounce) lobster tails,
   minced, shell discarded
1/3 bunch parsley, washed,
   drained, and finely chopped
1 cup Parmegiano Reggiano
   cheese, shredded

Clean and scrape the corn, being sure to get all of the milk out of the cobs.

Melt the butter in a large heavy-bottomed pot over medium heat. Add diced onions and sweat until they are translucent, about 3 to 5 minutes.

Mix the flour, sugar, Old Bay, and cayenne pepper together in a small bowl. Add this mixture to the onions. Stir to make a roux. Add cream and stir until thickened and mixture is thoroughly heated. Add Tabasco, lobster base, and brandy, and stir to incorporate. Add corn and stir to coat with roux.

Reduce heat and cook until corn kernels are tender, seasoning with salt and pepper until desired flavor is achieved. Remove from heat, transfer to a large container and refrigerate until cold.

When fully chilled, fold in meat from the lobster tail and the minced parsley. Transfer the mixture to a large casserole dish, or to individual service containers. Sprinkle generously with the Parmegiano Reggiano and place in an oven that has been preheated to 350 degrees. Cook 20 minutes, or until thoroughly heated and the cheese is melted and slightly browned on top.

Serve immediately.

TEXAS SHRIMP AND SAUSAGE WITH CREAMY GRITS

Bonnell's Fine Texas Cuisine, Fort Worth

Serves 4 to 6

Grits

1/2 cup chopped onion
1 teaspoon chopped garlic
1 teaspoon butter
2 teaspoons Frank's RedHot Sauce
1 cup heavy cream
1 cup chicken stock
2 tablespoons Creole Seasoning
  Blend *(see recipe, p. 117)*
1/2 cup Homestead Gristmill Grits
1/2 cup plus 2 tablespoons Monterey
  Jack cheese, grated

Shrimp and Sausage

2 links hot Andouille sausage
1 teaspoon butter
12 to 14 large (16 to 20 count)
  shrimp, peeled and deveined
1/2 cup heavy cream
1 teaspoon Franks RedHot Sauce
Salt and pepper to taste

To make the grits, sauté the onion and garlic in butter until soft. Add hot sauce, cream, and stock and bring to a simmer (the stage just before a rolling boil). Be careful not to let the liquids boil over. Quickly whisk in seasoning and grits while simmering. Stir constantly until grits begin to thicken; about 15 to 20 minutes. Turn heat to low. Gently fold in cheese and let grits sit for at least 5 minutes.

Dice the sausage into small cubes, then sauté in butter in a large skillet until slightly browned. Add the shrimp and cook over medium heat for 1 minute. Add cream and hot sauce and reduce sauce until it thickens. Season with salt and pepper and then pour pan over the grits and serve hot.

FRIED TOMATOES

Killen's Steakhouse, Pearland

Serves 4 to 6

Sauce
2 shallots, chopped
1/2 cup white wine
1 pound blended Roma tomatoes
1 cup heavy cream
2 tablespoons butter
2 tablespoons flour

Fried Tomatoes
1 pound Roma tomatoes,
  peeled and quartered
1 cup flour
1 cup buttermilk
Panko bread crumbs
Oil for frying

To make the sauce, bring chopped shallots, wine, and blended Roma tomatoes to a boil in a medium saucepan. Allow to reduce by half. Add heavy cream. Bring to boil and then strain.

To make a roux, mix butter and flour in a skillet over low heat and stir just until combined. Add roux to thicken to desired consistency.

Place peeled and quartered Roma tomatoes on paper towels to drain.

In separate bowls, place flour and buttermilk for battering. Dredge Roma tomatoes in flour and dip in buttermilk. Coat in Panko and fry in enough oil to cover until crispy. Serve hot, topped with sauce or served on the side.

GREEN CHILI AND PEARL ONION RAJAS

Smoke, at the Belmont Hotel, Dallas

Serves 8

4 Poblano chile peppers, roasted and peeled
2 dry Pasilla chilies, toasted, stem & seed removed
1 1/2 tablespoons vegetable oil
1/2 cup (8 ounces) pearl onions, blanched and peeled
1 clove garlic, minced
1/2 cup sour cream
1/2 teaspoon dry Mexican oregano
1/2 teaspoon dry marjoram
1 teaspoon fresh thyme, chopped, stems removed
8 bay leaves
Kosher salt to taste
3 teaspoons lime juice

Slice roasted Poblanos into 1/4-inch strips.

Rough chop the toasted dry Pasilla chilies or crush with a mortar and pestle.

Heat the oil in a heavy sauté pan over medium heat and fry the onions until they brown, about 7 to 8 minutes. Stir in garlic and cook 2 minutes. Add the roasted and dried chilies. Add the cream, herbs and bay leaf and simmer until the liquid reduces enough to just coat the vegetables.

Remove the bay leaf and adjust seasoning with salt to taste. Stir in lime juice and serve with chopped BBQ Beef Brisket *(see recipe, p. 80)*, roasted potatoes and a poached egg.

TIP
Rajas *means "strips of chilies." It's served with meat or as a vegetable side dish.*

BOHANAN'S BAKED EGGPLANT

Bohanan's Prime Steaks & Seafood, San Antonio

Serves 8

4 large eggplants, peeled and cut into 3/4-inch cubes
8 strips Berkshire (Kurobuta) bacon, thickly sliced
1/4 cup extra virgin Spanish olive oil
1 tablespoon granulated garlic
1 tablespoon granulated onion
2 bunches green onions, sliced thinly
Salt and freshly ground black pepper to taste

Topping
4 cups fresh bread crumbs, coarsely ground
1/4 cup Spanish extra virgin olive oil
1/4 cup freshly chopped herb mix (thyme, parsley, rosemary, oregano)
Salt and freshly ground black pepper to taste
1/2 cup Parmegiano Reggiano cheese, grated

Heat oven to 350 degrees. In a large heavy-bottomed pan over medium heat, cook the bacon until crispy. Remove the strips to paper towels and allow them to cool. Drain grease from the pan.

Pour the olive oil into the pan and heat over medium heat. As the oil heats, chop the bacon very finely. Add the bacon to the olive oil and simmer 1 minute to infuse the oil.

Add the eggplant to the pan. Add the seasonings and stir to coat the eggplant well. Cook the eggplant over medium heat until it begins to soften and the sides turn lightly golden. Add the green onions to the pan and stir briefly to just barely cook the onions. Test the eggplant for seasoning and adjust if needed. Transfer the eggplant mixture to a large prepared casserole dish.

For the topping, combine the bread crumbs, olive oil, herbs, salt, and pepper. Toss the ingredients until the bread crumbs are well coated. Sprinkle an even layer of the bread crumb mixture over the eggplant. Top the casserole with a dusting of the Parmegiano Reggiano cheese.

Place the dish in the preheated oven. Cook the eggplant until the topping is golden brown, the cheese has formed a nice crust and until the internal temperature has reached 165 degrees.

Remove from the oven and serve immediately.

Mon Dieu! Prime Time in Texas

The good news: We're Number 1! We Texans like to announce our primacy at the drop of a Stetson, and when it comes to beef we aren't exaggerating: Beef "R" Us. There was even a time (around 1825) when cattle outranked people in Texas twenty-two to one. As of January, 2010, Texas ranked first nationally in the number of cattle operations, the number of cattle, and the value of cattle ($10.5 million, if you are counting). In fact, according to the Texas Beef Council, raising cattle is a family affair: more than 97% of all cattle ranches in the U.S. are family-owned.

They're not that lucrative, either. You can expect to gross around $60,000 annually if you decide to get into the cattle-raising business. Apparently the modest income is not a deterrent in Texas because the cattle business is everywhere. All 254 counties have beef cattle operations, but the largest cattle inventory is in Deaf Smith County with 557,000 head. Not surprisingly, the county seat of Deaf Smith County is Hereford, named after the hardy breed of cattle popular with ranchers in the Southwest.

We even teach "meat" here in Texas. The Animal Science program at Texas A & M in College Station has been going strong for over a century. It's got competitive teams, just like their football program, except that the meat teams have done quite a bit better. They've garnered 15 national championships, whereas the A &M football team has only come out on top one-and-a-half times (in 1919 they went undefeated and unscored upon, but were one of three teams awarded the national title; in 1939 they went undefeated and were named national champions).

At Texas Tech in Lubbock, you can enroll in the Meat Science Department where you will study to be a meat scientist and become qualified to go to work for the United States Department of Agriculture. It's a job that focuses on the intricacies of amino acids and mono-unsaturated fats, but these professionals also struggle to define the indefinable: flavor, succulence, and satisfaction. Beef Sensory Evaluators eat a lot of steak all day long. Their goal is to categorize each steak using four attributes: juiciness, tenderness, cohesiveness, and characterization. Characterization is a complex category and includes sub-attributes: sweet, acid, sour, rancid, and warmed over. The analyses require interpretative skill, even though one conclusion has triumphed over and over. Marbling is the reason a steak tastes good. It all boils down to fat.

> **The stereotype is that steak is purely Texan, but a good case can be made that in France, steak is *le roi.* Think of the familiar names for cuts of beef that we must credit the French: *filet, filet mignon, tournedo, entrecote,* and *chateaubriand.***

We are now accustomed to believe that meat and the fat that comes with it is bad. But there are those—the late Marvin Harris, a cultural anthropologist of some note—who dare to be contrarians. Harris believes that humans are engineered to crave meat. In his book *Good to Eat: Riddles of Food & Culture*, he coined the term "meat hunger" to describe a basic longing that's built into our DNA. Texas steak lovers understand this concept. It's why the fancy new urban steakhouses pad their menus with luscious, fat-filled side dishes. Perhaps the most no-frills approach to gorging on fat reaches its pinnacle at the Big Texan Steak Ranch in Amarillo. The ambitiously hungry are encouraged to order the 72-ounce steak. That's four-and-a-half pounds. It's free if you can consume it in an hour, and a bucket comes with your order, in case—well, you can imagine.

On the topic of social etiquette, though, consider the French, whose notions of cooking and eating are notoriously dominant. The stereotype is that steak is purely Texan, but a good case can be made that in France, steak is *le roi*. Think of the familiar names for cuts of beef that we must credit the French: filet, filet mignon, tournedo, entrecote, and chateaubriand. Then, too, there's that Gallic dare-devil attitude towards eating. The French, as we know from their celebration of foie gras, have never shied away from fat. One of the most readily available dishes in France is steak frites, steak and fries that can be had at fine restaurants as readily as at service stops on the highways. And don't forget steak tartare, proof that the French love steak so much they'll eat it raw.

In *Mastering the Art of French Cooking*, Julia Child's recipe for pan-fried steaks is considered incomparable. She updated her recipe for steak au poivre with Jacques Pepin in *Julia and Jacques Cooking at Home*. Julia said it best when she quipped, "The only time to eat diet food is when you're waiting for the steak to cook."

Chefs the world over are getting their apron strings all in a knot trying to compete with Texas steak cuisine. Probably the most famous steak recipe from across the big pond belongs to the renowned French chef Alain Ducasse. It's available on his website and has been reprinted many times. But my au jus-stained copy was handed to me by my favorite backyard cooks. Gary Wilson and his wife LuAnn Bordelon are instinctive food enthusiasts who love meat and both swear that this recipe simply can't be topped. A steak cook book wouldn't be worth its salt without Ducasse's steady directions for success—which, by the way, validates the time-honored cooking traditions of Texas cooks: keep it simple.

The essential ingredient is a 2-pound boneless ribeye steak—it's just right for two people. Embellishments are kept at a spartan minimum: unsalted butter, unpeeled and crushed garlic, freshly ground pepper, and—*voila!*—a sprig of thyme. Cook 10 minutes on each side over medium heat, then set the delicacies aside in a warm place to rest for 10 or 15 minutes before serving. Chef Ducasse would like us to pair the dish with Swiss chard and an accompaniment of peppered cranberry marmalade (these recipes are also on his website), but diners used to cole slaw and a baked potato as sides may be driven to stomp their boots in protest. The sprig of thyme recommended as a decorative element may be pushing macho tolerance about as far as it can go.   —H.T.

SOUTH TEXAS ALBONDIGAS

Grady's Restaurant, Fort Worth

Makes 20 to 35

3 pounds sirloin ground beef
3 eggs, beaten
4 jalapeños, seeded and diced
1 red onion, diced
4 cloves of garlic, minced
1 bunch cilantro, chopped
1/2 cup tomato paste
2 tablespoons brown sugar
1 cup grated Monterey Jack cheese
Kosher salt to taste

This is one of Grady's modern twists on a cowboy classic—albondigas (meaning, literally, meatballs) so good you can eat them for dinner. Here and at his restaurants, Grady serves them as an appetizer.

Preheat the oven to 375 degrees.

In a large mixing bowl, thoroughly combine all the ingredients by hand. Divide the mixture into balls, rolling them in your hand until they are firm and just slightly smaller than the size of a golf ball. Place the Albondigas on an oiled baking sheet and cook for 20 to 25 minutes, or until done.

HOMINY CASSEROLE

Smoke, at the Belmont Hotel, Dallas

Serves 10 to 12

1 cup yellow corn grits, stone ground, coarse
1/2 cup yellow cornmeal, medium grind
1/2 cup yellow corn polenta flour
1 cup rendered chopped bacon
1 teaspoon black peppercorn, crushed
1 quart chicken or ham stock
1/2 cup heavy cream
1/4 cup chopped pickled jalapeño
1 cup white corn hominy
2 tablespoons pickled jalapeño vinegar
2 1/2 cups sharp cheddar cheese, shredded
1/2 cup sour cream
2 teaspoons kosher salt
1 tablespoon Louisiana Hot Sauce

Using old-fashioned ingredients and methods of cooking that hark back to country kitchens, smokehouses and outdoor barbecue pits, Chef Tim Byres's dishes are pure comfort food.

In a medium bowl mix the grits, cornmeal and polenta flour together and set aside.

Heat a heavy-bottomed pot on medium-high heat and add the bacon and black pepper. Render the bacon until crispy but not burned. Slowly add the stock and heavy cream and bring to a simmer.

Whisk in the dry cornmeal mixture in three parts, until completely incorporated; then reduce heat to low and continue to stir until mixture is thick and smooth. (The coarse grind cornmeal should be cooked until soft, about 15 minutes.)

Fold in the hominy and pickled jalapeño vinegar and slowly cook until the grits are set. Remove the pot from the stove and fold in the sour cream, 2 cups cheddar cheese, salt, and Louisiana Hot Sauce.

Preheat boiler. Pour grits into one large or 12 small casserole dishes and sprinkle with reserved cheddar cheese. Broil until golden brown.

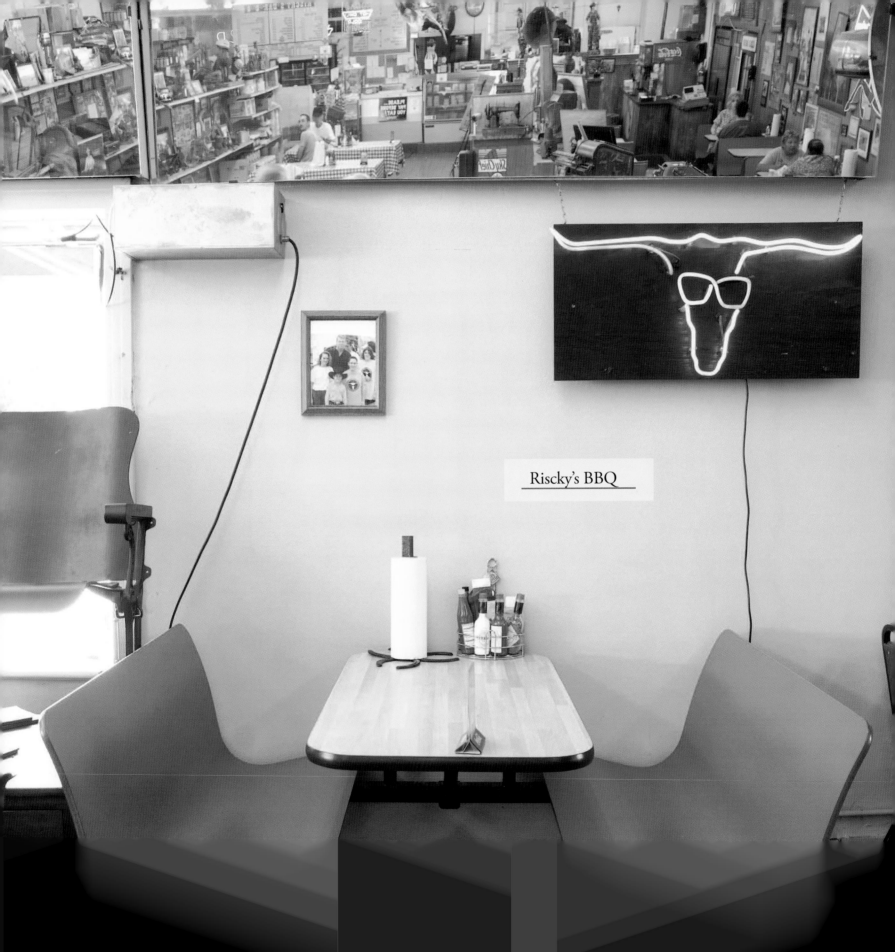

Riscky's BBQ

Del Frisco's Double Eagle Steak House

ROQUEFORT PORT COMPOUND BUTTER

Taste of Texas Restaurant, Houston

Makes 1 quart

4 ounces Roquefort, broken into
small pieces
1 stick unsalted butter
1 teaspoon Dijon mustard

½ ounce Ruby Port wine
1 teaspoon minced garlic
Pinch of ground white pepper

With all ingredients at room temperature, fold together in a medium bowl until just combined. Try to leave Roquefort pieces intact. Using a large sheet of parchment paper, make a 1 1/2-inch diameter roll and refrigerate for at least 2 hours.

When ready to use, unroll from parchment and cut 1/2-inch pats of butter, using a sharp knife. Allow one pat of butter per steak and top steak with butter as it comes from the grill.

RANCHMAN'S STEAK BUTTER

Ranchman's Ponder Steakhouse, Ponder

Serves 8

1 stick (1/2 pound) butter, softened
2 teaspoons salt
2 teaspoons pepper
1 teaspoon garlic granules
1 lemon, juiced

In large mixing bowl, combine butter and all other ingredients. Use a mixer set on low speed to begin, then gradually increase the speed. Be sure to stop mixer and scrape sides of bowl each time you change the speed. Whip until the butter is the consistency of whipped cream. It will triple in volume.

Spread a rounded tablespoon of Steak Butter on top of your cooked steak. Cover and refrigerate to store.

BUCKAROO SAUCE

Big Texan Steak Ranch, Amarillo

Mkes 1 1/2 pints

2 cups chili sauce, your favorite brand
8 teaspoons grated horseradish
1 lemon, juiced
20 dashes Worcestershire sauce

20 dashes Tabasco
10 dashes Frank's RedHot Sauce
1 teaspoon season salt
1/4 cup dried chopped chives

Mix ingredients well. Chill in refrigerator for at least two hours before serving.

RICH CHICKEN BROTH

Reata Restaurant, Fort Worth

5 chicken legs and thighs
Water
4 shallots, peeled
1 whole head garlic, peeled

2 carrots
1 tablespoon black peppercorns
Kosher salt
Freshly ground black pepper

To make the chicken broth, place the chicken in a large, heavy stockpot with a lid. Add the water, shallots, garlic, carrots, and peppercorns. The liquid should just barely cover the chicken, so adjust the depth of the water, if needed. Cook over medium-high heat and bring the mixture to a boil. As the liquid begins to heat, skim off the foam that rises to the surface, and discard. When it begins to boil, lower the heat to a constant simmer.

Continue skimming as needed. Cover the pot, leaving the lid slightly ajar, and continue cooking for 90 minutes. Remove the pot from the heat, and leave the chicken in the broth for 30 minutes to cool.

When the chicken is cool enough to handle, remove the skin and bones and discard. Shred the remaining chicken (should make about 3 cups) and reserve in a covered container to use later. Strain the remaining broth, there should be about 2 quarts, and return to a clean saucepan. Skim off any fat that accumulates on the surface. Season with salt and pepper.

SOUTHWESTERN SEASONING BLEND

Bonnell's Fine Texas Cuisine, Fort Worth

Makes about 1 cup

5 tablespoons iodized salt
2 tablespoons granulated garlic
2 tablespoons fine black pepper
2 teaspoons cayenne pepper
3/4 tablespoon dried thyme
3/4 tablespoon dried oregano
2 tablespoons paprika

1 tablespoon onion powder
1/2 tablespoon dried basil
1/2 tablespoon cumin
2 teaspoons coriander
2 tablespoons chili powder
1/2 tablespoon dry mustard powder

Toss all ingredients together in a bowl and store in an airtight container until ready to apply to meat before cooking.

WILDCATTER STEAK RUB

Wildcatter Ranch Steakhouse, Graham

Makes 1 1/2 cups

1/3 cup beef base, powder or paste
1 tablespoon kosher salt
1/2 cup coarse black pepper
1 tablespoon cornstarch
2 tablespoons oregano
1/2 cup paprika

1 tablespoon dry thyme leaves
1 teaspoon onion powder
1 teaspoon cinnamon
1 teaspoon granulated garlic
1 tablespoon dry minced garlic

Mix together in a small bowl and refrigerate until ready to use.

FORT GRIFFIN STORE RUB

Fort Griffin General Merchandise Company, Albany

Makes 3 pints

1 cup kosher salt
1 cup black pepper
1 cup garlic powder
1 cup ground oregano
1 cup onion powder
1 cup parsley
2 teaspoons cinnamon
2 teaspoons nutmeg

Combine all ingredients in a food processor and thoroughly blend.

Rub can be used for your favorite steak, chicken, or pork. Keep refrigerated. This recipe can be halved.

CHILI RUB AND COFFEE CURE

Smoke, at the Belmont Hotel, Dallas

Makes 1 pint

1/3 cup chili powder
1/3 cup smoked paprika
2 tablespoons granulated garlic
1 tablespoon ground cumin
1 teaspoon cayenne pepper, finely ground

1/2 cup kosher salt
2/3 cup dark brown sugar
3 tablespoons granulated sugar
1/3 cup dark roast coffee, finely ground

Combine all ingredients. Rub can be stored in a 1-quart mason jar.

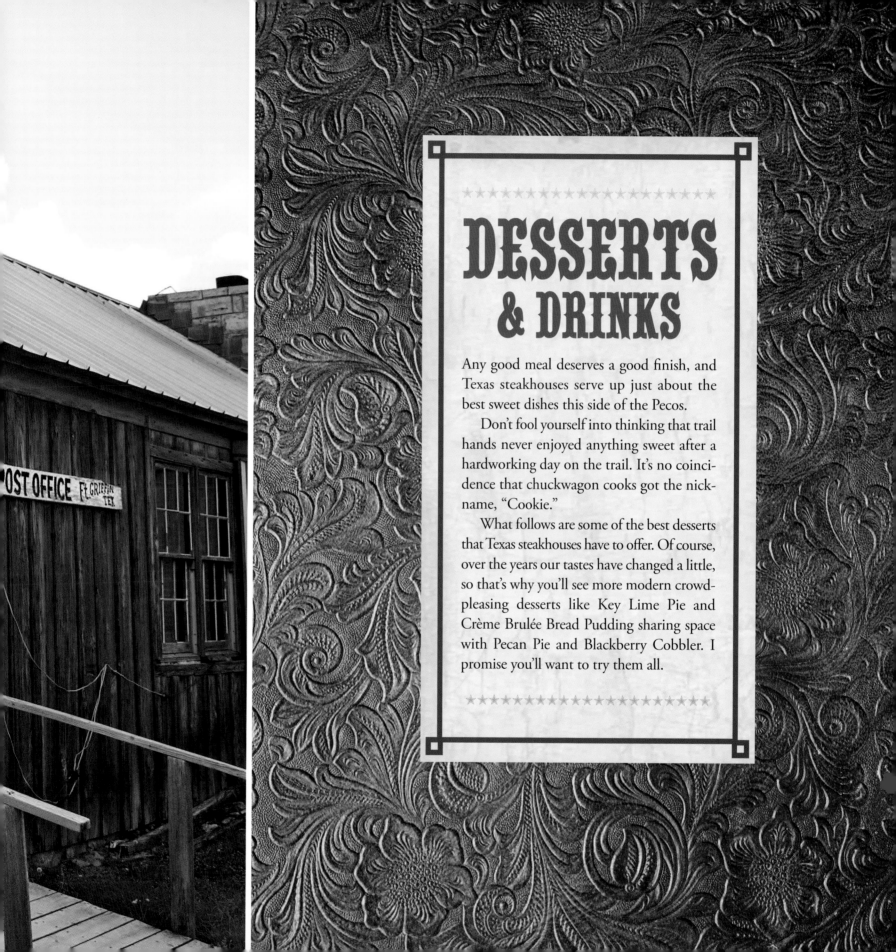

DESSERTS & DRINKS

Any good meal deserves a good finish, and Texas steakhouses serve up just about the best sweet dishes this side of the Pecos.

Don't fool yourself into thinking that trail hands never enjoyed anything sweet after a hardworking day on the trail. It's no coincidence that chuckwagon cooks got the nickname, "Cookie."

What follows are some of the best desserts that Texas steakhouses have to offer. Of course, over the years our tastes have changed a little, so that's why you'll see more modern crowd-pleasing desserts like Key Lime Pie and Crème Brulée Bread Pudding sharing space with Pecan Pie and Blackberry Cobbler. I promise you'll want to try them all.

HOMEMADE BREAD PUDDING WITH HONEY BOURBON SAUCE

Fort Griffin General Merchandise Company, Albany

Serves 8

3 eggs
1 pint plus 1/2 cup heavy whipping cream
1 tablespoon pure vanilla extract
3 teaspoons cinnamon
1 teaspoon nutmeg
1 cup sugar
4 cups Bavarian bread, cut into 1-inch cubes (or, pumpernickel can be substituted)
6 cups French boule bread, cut into 1-inch cubes (or, sourdough bread can be substituted)

Honey Bourbon Sauce
(makes 9 ounces)
1 stick of unsalted butter
1 measured shot Wild Turkey American Honey Whiskey (or, Wild Turkey Kentucky Whiskey may be substituted)
1 cup honey

This steakhouse, housed in a former turn-of-the-century general merchandise store, is the best reason I can think of to travel 135 miles from Dallas for a meal.

Owners Ali and Nariman Esfandiary have created a successful restaurant with the charm and appeal of the real Wild West. Dishes like this homemade bread pudding are your prize at the end of a great meal.

Preheat oven to 350 degrees. Spray a 9-inch glass baking dish with non-stick cooking spray.

In a bowl, mix eggs, 1 pint of heavy whipping cream, vanilla, cinnamon, nutmeg, and sugar and set aside.

Lay 3 cups of French bread in bottom of baking dish. Next, lay the Bavarian bread in the center, then place remaining boule bread on top. Pour the mixture over the bread in the baking dish. Gently press the bread, making sure all pieces are covered with the mixture. Let the dish settle for a few minutes, then place in the oven.

Cook for 20 minutes, then rotate the dish and cook another 20 minutes. Remove from oven, place in refrigerator to settle and cool for 2 hours.

To serve, run a knife around outer edge, pulling knife in, away from dish. Serve with Honey Bourbon Sauce (see below). To serve hot, place the dish in oven for 10 minutes at 350 degrees.

To make the sauce, melt butter in saucepan over medium heat. Once melted, remove from heat, and stir in honey, then whiskey. Heat sauce over low heat for several minutes, or place in a microwavable dish and microwave for 25 seconds.

DUBLIN DR. PEPPER FLOAT WITH CINNAMON BUNUELO COOKIES

Bonnell's Fine Texas Cuisine, Fort Worth

Serves 1

Cookies
2 flour tortillas
2 quarts canola oil
2 tablespoons sugar
1/2 teaspoon ground cinnamon

Float
1 bottle Dublin Original Dr. Pepper
2 scoops premium vanilla ice cream
2 to 3 tablespoons whipped cream

This Dr. Pepper comes directly from the original factory in Dublin, Texas—sometimes referred to as Dr. Pepper, Texas. These drinks are made from the original formula for Dr. Pepper, using Imperial Pure Cane Sugar.

The story goes that when the owner of the Dublin bottling plant, Bill Kloster, was told by his wife that he ought to drink diet Dr. Pepper to limit his sugar intake, he had the real Dr. Pepper formula put into diet bottles just for him to stock in his home refrigerator.

This is the kind of float that will make you a fan of Dr. Pepper forever.

To make the cookies, cut the tortillas into any shape desired. (At Bonnell's, they are shaped into stars and the state of Texas using cookie cutters. They can also be cut into thin strips for garnish.) Mix the sugar and cinnamon together. In vegetable oil heated to 350 degrees, fry the tortillas until crispy. Remove and drain on paper towels. While the tortillas are still hot and fresh from the oil, sprinkle with cinnamon sugar mixture to coat.

To assemble the float, freeze a glass prior to making the float. Place 2 scoops of ice cream into the frosted glass and then slowly pour in the Dr. Pepper. To serve, top with whipped cream and Cinnamon Bunuelo Cookies, or your choice.

CRÈME BRULÉE BREAD PUDDING

Killen's Steakhouse, Pearland

Serves 5

Chosen by Food & Wine *magazine in 2008 as one of the 10 best dishes in America, this luscious dessert tastes complicated but is really easy to make.*

3 French baguettes
1/2 cup dried apricots, julienned
1/2 pint blueberries
1 quart heavy whipping cream
5 egg yolks
1 cup granulated sugar
1/4 tablespoon vanilla paste
Bread Pudding Sauce

Bread Pudding Sauce
8 Granny Smith apples, cored
   and sliced
1/4 pound (1/2 stick) unsalted butter
2 3/4 cups dark brown sugar
1 cup raisins
1 1/2 each cinnamon sticks
1/2 teaspoon ground cinnamon
1/2 cup brandy

Preheat oven to 275 degrees.

In a saucepan, heat whipping cream and vanilla until scalding.

Break French baguette into 2-inch pieces and place in a large baking pan. Add julienned apricots and blueberries.

In a large bowl, thoroughly combine the sugar and egg yolks. Temper the whipping cream mixture into the egg yolk mixture, adding a little at a time until incorporated. Pour the custard mixture into the baking pan and mix. Let sit for 10 minutes until the bread absorbs the mixture. Stir as needed so that all custard is absorbed.

Bake at 275 degrees for 1 hour. Increase temperature to 300 degrees and bake 10 to 15 minutes longer, or until a light golden brown color is reached.

Remove from oven and let cool to room temperature before refrigerating. Serve with Bread Pudding Sauce.

To make the sauce, sauté the apples in butter in a large saucepan until almost soft. Add brown sugar, raisins, cinnamon sticks, and brandy. Stirring, simmer for 15 minutes. Refrigerate until needed.

BLACKBERRY COBBLER

Ranchman's Ponder Steakhouse, Ponder

2 pounds frozen blackberries
3 cups water
2 cups sugar
8 ounces roux, *(see recipe, p. 174)*
1/2 teaspoon red food coloring
Ranchman's Pastry Dough, prepared
   in advance

Ranchman's Pastry Dough
*(makes 2 double crust pies, or two
   cobblers)*
1/2 pound vegetable shortening
3 1/2 cups all-purpose flour
1/2 tablespoon salt
1/2 cup cold water

Preheat oven to 350 degrees.

In a saucepan, combine water, sugar, and a handful of blackberries. Bring to a boil and add roux and red food coloring. Continue to boil, whisking constantly until sauce thickens. Make sure that there are no roux lumps remaining.

Place remaining frozen blackberries in an 11 x14-inch, deep-dish casserole. Pour thickened, hot sauce over top.

To make the pastry, place all ingredients in the bowl of a mixer fitted with the paddle attachment. Blend just until well-mixed, approximately 1 minute. Do not over-mix. Remove dough from mixing bowl and form into 4 patties, wrapping each separately in plastic-wrap, and refrigerate until needed. Let dough come to room temperature before rolling out for pies. Note: You will need 1 ounce of dough for every 1-inch diameter of your pie pan. In other words, for a 10-inch pie pan, you will need 10 ounces of dough.

To bake the pie crusts, be sure to roll out dough using plenty of flour to keep it from sticking. Place raw dough in pie pan, place a pie pan on top of dough and cut off edges that hang over. Leaving the pan inside the dough pan, bake both together in a preheated 350 degree oven for one hour, or until golden brown. Remove from oven and carefully lift off the inserted pan to let cool. Pastry dough should rest at room temperature after baking.

Roll out pastry dough a little thicker than you would a pie dough, about 1/4-inch thickness, and cut into strips, each about 1-inch width. Weave strips to cover cobbler, spacing strips 1/4-inch apart, making two layers. Let dough strips run up the side of casserole about 1/2 inch.

Bake for 1 hour, or until crust is golden brown.

Cobblers are time-honored traditional fare in this part of the country, their goodness dependent only on the berry crops and the size of your appetite. You'll want seconds with this one.

DEEP DISH KEY LIME PIE

Taste of Texas Restaurant, Houston

Serves 10

2 cups fresh Key lime juice
5 (14-ounce cans) Eagle Brand
  sweetened condensed milk
16 fresh egg yolks
2 (16-ounce) containers sour cream
2 cups heavy whipping cream
1 3/4 cups powdered sugar
1 graham cracker crust, in a deep
  dish pie shell
Fresh raspberries or raspberry puree
  to garnish

Graham Cracker Pie Shell
1/2 stick salted butter, melted
2 cups graham cracker crumbs
1/3 cup granulated sugar
1 tablespoon vanilla extract

Preheat oven to 325 degrees.

To make the pie shell, combine all ingredients in a standing mixer until fully incorporated. Note: The only way to hurt this pie shell is to under-mix the ingredients. Using the flat palm of your hand, press 1 cup of the mixture into the sides of a 10-inch deep dish pie shell first, using your fingers to compress the mixture. Once you've finished all the sides, press one cup mixture into the bottom of the pan, making sure the mixture is pressed evenly throughout the pie shell.

In a standing mixer, whip the condensed milk on medium speed for 2 minutes. Add the egg yolks slowly, in three parts, and whip until combined. Add the lime juice in a slow, steady stream, and continue mixing for another 2 minutes. Note: It is important to add the egg yolks to the sweetened condensed milk before the lime juice. The acid in the lime juice will curdle the egg yolks if they are not given time to mix with the sugar.

Pour the mixture into a prepared pie shell and bake for 10 minutes. Remove the pie from the oven, evenly spread sour cream over the pie and return to the oven for another 15 minutes. Turn the oven off and let the pie rest in the oven with the door closed for another 15 minutes.

Remove the pie from the oven and refrigerate overnight. When ready to serve, whip together the heavy cream and powdered sugar to make whipped cream. Top the pie with a generous layer of whipped cream, garnish with raspberries or a drizzle of raspberry puree, and serve.

RANCHMAN'S COCONUT PIE

Ranchman's Ponder Steakhouse, Ponder

Serves 6 to 8

1 teaspoon flour
2 egg yolks, beaten
2 1/2 cups milk
1 cup sugar
4 ounces roux
1 1/2 teaspoons vanilla
1 cup coconut
Meringue
Pre-baked pie shell, or see
  Ranchman's Pastry Dough *(see p. 171)*

Roux
3/4 stick butter or margarine
1/2 cup and 1 tablespoon flour

Meringue
1/2 cup egg whites
1/4 teaspoon of cream of
  tartar
1/3 cup sugar
1/4 teaspoon vanilla

This pie seems to be on the menu every day at Ranchman's. One taste will tell you why—you just don't get straightforward, old-fashioned pies like this often enough these days. Dig in!

Preheat oven to 325 degrees.

To prepare the roux, stir the butter and flour together in a saucepan or skillet over medium heat until the flour thickens but does not brown. Cook until you can no longer taste the raw flour, but remove from heat before the roux begins to color.

In a saucepan, mix together beaten egg yolks, milk, flour, and sugar. Heat on medium-high until steaming, or just barely boiling. Add the roux, stirring continuously with wire whisk until smooth and thick. Remove from heat and stir in the coconut and vanilla.

While mixture is still hot, transfer to pre-baked pie shell. Have meringue ready to beat and top it while the filling is hot.

To make the meringue, beat egg whites on high until foamy. Add cream of tartar and 1/3 of the sugar and beat until soft peaks form. Using a mixer set on high, add the remaining sugar until sugar dissolves and glossy peaks form. Whip in the vanilla and spoon onto pie.

Bake for 15 minutes, or until the filling is set and the meringue peaks are browned.

Ranchman's Ponder Steakhouse

APPLE BLONDIE

Bailey's Prime Plus, Fort Worth

Serves 8

1/2 pound unsalted butter
2 tablespoons vanilla extract
1 1/2 apples, peeled and sliced 1/8-inch thick
1 teaspoon lemon juice
1 tablespoon water
1/2 tablespoon white sugar
1 pound plus 1/2 tablespoon light brown sugar
Pinch ginger
1/4 teaspoon cinnamon
2 cups all-purpose flour
2 teaspoons baking powder
Small pinch salt
2 eggs
1 cup chopped pecans

Bailey's prides itself on its world-class dessert menu, and this is one of the stars. Not an apple pie, this recipe thoroughly melds the ingredients into a rich, sweet dessert square. Made with flour, brown sugar, butter, eggs, baking powder, and vanilla, the dominant flavor of any blondie recipe is the brown sugar. They are sometimes called "blonde brownies," although they contain no chocolate.

Preheat oven to 325 degrees.

In a large saucepan over medium-low heat, melt butter, 1 pound brown sugar, and vanilla extract, but do not allow mixture to boil.

Place lemon juice and water in a mixing bowl. Cut apple slices in half. Place into bowl and mix with water and lemon juice to keep the apples from oxidizing. Toss with the white sugar, 1 tablespoon brown sugar, ground ginger, and cinnamon. Set aside.

In a small bowl, combine the flour, baking powder, and salt. Using a separate bowl, alternately stir in the flour mixture and the eggs, using a whisk to incorporate. Stir in the pecans.

Drain the excess liquid from the apples and fold into the flour mixture.

Pour mixture into well-greased casserole and bake for 30 minutes. Let cool completely. Cut into rounds using a 3-inch cookie cutter, or slice into squares and serve with your favorite ice cream or caramel sauce.

PATTIE'S POUNDCAKE WITH RASPBERRY CHAMBORD SAUCE

Wildcatter Ranch Steakhouse, Graham

Serves 8

1 cup unsalted butter, at room temperature
2 cups sugar
1/2 teaspoon baking powder
1/2 teaspoon baking soda
4 eggs, beaten
2 teaspoons Mexican vanilla, or vanilla extract
2 teaspoons almond extract
1 cup buttermilk
3 cups flour, sifted twice
Raspberry Chambord Sauce

Raspberry Chambord Sauce
1 cup fresh raspberries
1 cup fresh blackberries
1 cup powdered sugar
1/4 cup Chambord (black raspberry liqueur)
3 tablespoons freshly squeezed lemon juice

Preheat oven to 350 degrees. Butter and lightly flour a bundt pan.

Cream the butter and sugar together. Add the baking powder, baking soda, eggs, vanilla, and almond extract. Gradually add the buttermilk and flour, alternately stirring in a little at a time. Pour into the prepared pan.

Bake for 1 hour, or until the cake is golden brown. Serve with Raspberry Chambord Sauce and garnish with fresh berries and whipped cream.

To make the sauce, mix all the ingredients together in a blender or food processor. Strain the mixture through a fine-mesh sieve to remove the seeds. Discard the seeds. Cover and refrigerate for at least 1 hour. Drizzle on plate as garnish or over warm pound cake.

STRAWBERRY SHORTCAKE

Perini Ranch Steakhouse, Buffalo Gap

Serves 8

2 pounds ripe strawberries
1/2 cup sugar
8 buttermilk biscuits *(recipe below)*,
    sweetened to taste
1 cup heavy cream

Buttermilk Biscuits
(makes 2 dozen biscuits)
2 cups flour
2 teaspoons baking powder
1/2 teaspoon baking soda
3/4 teaspoon salt
3 tablespoons vegetable shortening
1 cup buttermilk

Biscuits are the perfect "cake" element for strawberry short-cake—they are firm and dense enough to retain their shape and not become soggy in the sweet cream.

A suggestion: make the biscuits in the morning and you'll have enough left for this dessert that evening.

Remove tops from the strawberries and halve. Sprinkle with sugar and let sit at room temperature until they begin to produce juice. Put the strawberries and juice in a saucepan and warm thoroughly over very low heat, until the juice begins to thicken.

To make the biscuits, combine all dry ingredients. Add the shortening and mix well with the back of a mixing spoon. Add the buttermilk and mix thoroughly. Roll out dough on a floured board to 1/2-inch thickness. Cut into rounds and place on an ungreased baking sheet.

Bake biscuits for about 10 minutes, or until golden brown.

To assemble, slice the biscuits in half, spoon strawberries onto the bottom biscuit, then replace the top half and cover with another spoonful of strawberries. Top with heavy whipping cream.

BANANA PUDDING

Star Cafe, Fort Worth

Serves 4 to 6

2 cups milk, divided
3 eggs, separated, and egg whites discarded
1 cup regular white sugar, plus 2 to 3 tablespoons
3 heaping tablespoons all-purpose flour
Salt to taste
2 teaspoons vanilla
2 tablespoons butter or margarine, room temperature
1 box vanilla wafers
4 bananas, sliced into 1/8-inch rounds
1/2 pint heavy whipping cream

Located in the Historic Fort Worth Stockyards, the Star Cafe was built in the early 1900s and wears its charm like a Texas badge of honor. From the tin ceiling to the countertops, the Star Cafe offers a nostalgic trip to another era. Family owned and operated, the Star Cafe is dedicated to old-fashioned service and quality.

Heat 1 cup milk in top of a double boiler over gently boiling water. While the milk is warming, separate the eggs, placing the yolks into a small mixing bowl. Using a fork, beat the egg yolks until they are a lemon color. Gradually add 1 cup sugar, using a fork to beat. After sugar is incorporated, add flour, one tablespoon at a time, and 1 cup milk.

When the milk in the double boiler is hot, but not boiling, skim off the skin that has formed on top and discard it. Add the egg mixture to the hot milk, using a whisk to stir. Keep whisking the pudding while it cooks, stopping when the mixture has thickened.

Remove pudding from heat and add a few pinches of salt, the vanilla, and butter.

Layer vanilla wafers and bananas in a bowl, covering each layer with pudding. Repeat the layering, ending with a pudding layer to keep the bananas from turning brown. Allow the pudding to sit for 1 1/2 hours before serving.

To make a whipped cream topping, beat heavy whipping cream together with 2 to 3 tablespoons sugar until it holds together.

Spoon the pudding into individual serving dishes and top with a spoonful of whipped cream.

TUACA CHOCOLATE MILKSHAKE

Love Shack, Fort Worth

Serves 1

2 ounces chocolate ganache, or 1 ounce
  chocolate and 1 ounce heavy cream,
  beaten together
2 ounces Tuaca liquor
3/4 cup homemade chocolate ice cream
2 ounces whole milk

Mix all ingredients in a blender until thick and creamy.

COFFEE BANANAS FOSTER

Silver Fox Steakhouse, Fort Worth

Serves 4

1 ounce unsalted butter
1/4 cup Sugar in the Raw
4 bananas, peeled and sliced into 1/2-inch slices
2 ounces coffee liqueur flavoring
Vanilla ice cream
8 waffle wafers, or broken waffle cones

Melt butter in sauté pan over high heat. Working quickly, add Sugar in the Raw and cook until melted. Add banana slices and cook until bananas begin to brown. While this is cooking, scoop ice cream into bowls, and place waffle wafers on each side of the ice cream.

Add coffee liqueur flavoring to the pan with bananas, continue cooking until liquid reduces. Pour banana mixture over ice cream and serve immediately.

KAHLUA BANANAS FOSTER

Fort Griffin General Merchandise Company, Albany

Serves 4

2 bananas, cut into equal quarters
1/2 cup brown sugar, not packed
1/4 teaspoon pure vanilla
1/4 teaspoon ground cinnamon
1/2 measured shot Kahlua liqueur
3 teaspoons butter
2 pints vanilla ice cream

Melt butter over medium heat in a small saucepan. Add brown sugar, vanilla, cinnamon, and Kahlua to saucepan and reduce heat. Slice banana into even quarters and place in individual bowls. Place scoops of ice cream over bananas, pour sauce over ice cream, and serve immediately.

DESSERT TOSTADAS WITH ICE CREAM AND FRESH BERRIES

Grady's Restaurant, Fort Worth

Serves 6

Tostada Shells
1/2 cup brown sugar
1/2 cup (1 stick) unsalted butter
1 1/2 tablespoons corn syrup
1/2 tablespoon vanilla
1/2 cup flour

Filling
1 pint vanilla ice cream
1 cup caramelized bananas
1 cup finely diced strawberries
1/8 cup julienned mint leaves
1/8 cup grated white chocolate

Preheat the oven to 400 degrees.

Prepare the tostadas by combining the brown sugar, butter, corn syrup, and vanilla in a heavy saucepan over medium heat, stirring to combine. When the butter has melted and the sugar has dissolved, remove pan from the heat and whisk in the flour until it forms a caramel-colored paste. Set aside to cool.

Line a cookie sheet with parchment paper. Spread the tostada mixture over the paper-lined tray with a pastry knife or spatula, evenly coating the paper; the mixture should be almost transparent. Cook for 5 to 6 minutes in the oven, or until golden brown and bubbly. Remove from the oven and immediately cut 12 (3-inch diameter) rounds out of the mixture, using a biscuit cutter or a glass. Remove each round and set aside to cool.

To serve, place 2 tostadas on each plate. Top each tostada with a spoonful of ice cream, then the caramelized bananas, and finally the diced strawberries. Garnish with mint and grated white chocolate

Just one look, and clever Grady Spears has fooled us into thinking this is a taco, not a dessert. Never fear! Even the tostada shells are sweet and crispy enough to please any sweet tooth.

The Chuckwagon—A Studebaker?

Say It Ain't So, Cookie

Consider that trail drives made the long, arduous trip from the Texas trails to the railyards in Kansas and Missouri—some went even as far as Wyoming and Canada. Trail hands had to carry what they could with them, which wasn't much—such as dried beef, corn fritters or biscuits. So, Texas rancher Charles Goodnight came up with a bright idea and in 1886 designed the first prototype chuckwagon.

Goodnight used an army surplus Studebaker wagon for his model. The Studebaker was sturdy, with steel axles that could hold up over rough trails for up to a five-months drive (one wonders whether that guarantee was put in writing upon sale!). He added a boot to the rear of his wagon and a pantry or chuck box for the food to be stored. The chuck box was designed to contain a number of shelves and compartments to hold different foodstuffs—think of the rolltop desks from this era that seemed to have cubbyholes for everything. Some outfitters would supply large tenting that could be extended from the wagon providing cover over the cooking area and cowboys gathered around the fire.

Goodnight's simple invention revolutionized the cattle industry. A herd of about 3,000 head would take around 10 to 15 cowboys; this included the trail boss, the wrangler and the cook. With a chuckwagon, a cook could store enough to feed his crew for a drive that might last up to five months.

A hinged door concealing the supplies could drop down to provide a worktop for food preparation. The boot carried the Dutch ovens and cooking utensils, and the water barrels were attached to the sides of the wagon. A canvas tarp slung under the wagon held what kindling they could pick up along the trail. The average wagon box was only 10 feet long and 38 to 40 inches wide, so consider how much had to fit into this small space in order to feed the men. Just packing and unpacking it all every day must have been a devil of a chore that would invariably have taken the patience of a saint. Unfortunately, most didn't, which is why trail cooks are always portrayed in film and books as being... a bit touchy, shall we say?

When we imagine a chuckwagon, most people envision the Conestoga wagons of the westward migration, but those wagons were large freight wagons that measured up to 24 feet in length. A few made trail drives but they were not as popular as Studebaker, or Moline wagons—a company who had been building wagons since the 1850s—for the long drive. The Studebaker Wagon Company and the Moline Wagon Company seemed to lead the herd in production of chuckwagons, and it became such a popular vehicle that by the end of the great trail drives in the early 1900s, both companies were still selling pre-built "round-up" wagons.

The chuckwagon so historically represents the era of the trail drives and the cowboys who worked the cattle that it was honored in 2005 as the official Texas State Vehicle. The iconic chuckwagon continues operations on many ranches nearly 150 years after its invention. Online sales and auctions of antique chuckwagons are popular, and some are still used for catering and outdoor cooking competitions, so the romantic image of trail cooking is alive and well, not only in Texas, but throughout the country.   —J.S.

TRES LECHES CRÈME BRULÉE

Bonnell's Fine Texas Cuisine, Fort Worth

Serves 8

1 1/4 cups heavy cream
6 tablespoons sweetened condensed milk
6 tablespoons evaporated milk
1/2 cup brown sugar, divided
1/2 vanilla bean, scraped
Pinch of salt
4 egg yolks
2 tablespoons plus 2 teaspoons white
    sugar, divided
Berries for garnish (1 pint each, blueberries,
    blackberries, and strawberries)

Preheat oven to 325 degrees.

In a medium saucepan, heat cream, condensed milk, evaporated milk, ¼ cup brown sugar, and vanilla. Bring to a boil and then turn off the heat.

In a large mixing bowl, whisk together remaining brown sugar, salt, and egg yolks until smooth. While vigorously whisking, slowly pour hot cream mixture into bowl with eggs and sugar; begin with just a few drops and then slowly increase the flow of hot cream until it is fully incorporated. Note: It's very important to start slowly to keep the eggs from cooking. Be sure to keep whisking while the cream mixture is being poured. Strain the mixture to ensure no lumps have formed.

Pour into 8-ounce ramekins. Place the ramekins in a baking dish and the fill the dish with water halfway up the sides of the ramekins. Cover loosely with foil and bake for 45 to 60 minutes, or until mixture has just set. Refrigerate until cool.

Just prior to serving, sprinkle a teaspoon of sugar over the top of each and spread evenly. Burn the sugar with a kitchen blowtorch until the sugar has melted and turned light brown. Top with a few berries to garnish and serve.

PECAN PIE

Cattlemen's Steak House, Fort Worth

Serves 6 to 8

3 eggs, slightly beaten
3/4 cup light corn syrup
3/4 cup sugar
2 tablespoons melted butter
1 teaspoon vanilla
1 tablespoon flour
Pinch each of salt and cinnamon
1 1/2 cups chopped pecans
Pie shell

Preheat oven to 350 degrees.

Thoroughly mix all ingredients, folding in the pecans last. Pour into a prepared pie shell and bake for 50 to 55 minutes. Allow to cool slightly before serving.

BONNELL'S BRANDY ICE

Bonnell's Fine Texas Cuisine, Fort Worth

Serves 3

1 1/4 ounces brandy
3/4 ounce Kahlua
3/4 ounce white Crème de Cocoa
1 ounce Godiva white chocolate liqueur
1 ounce heavy cream
2 scoops vanilla ice cream, your
    favorite brand
3 scoops cinnamon ice cream, your
    favorite brand

Garnish
Chocolate shavings
Ground cinnamon

Combine all wet ingredients in a glass. Using a bar blender, add the ice cream first, then pour the wet ingredients over, and blend until smooth. Pour into a brandy snifter and garnish with a dash of ground cinnamon and a sprinkle of chocolate shavings.

TEXAS SUNSET

Bonnell's Fine Texas Cuisine, Fort Worth

Serves 1

2 1/2 ounces Bacardi Limon
1 ounce Cointreau
1 lemon wedge, juice only
1/2 ounce cranberry juice
1/2 ounce gold tequila
3/4 ounce grenadine
Twist of lemon

Mix all ingredients except for grenadine in a bar shaker with one scoop of ice and shake well to chill. Strain well, and pour into a chilled martini glass. Pour the grenadine in last to achieve that "perfect sunset" look. Garnish with a twist of lemon.

SMOKE'S MARGARITA

Smoke, at the Belmont Hotel, Dallas

Serves 8

2 ounces Cedar Wood-Infused Jose Cuervo
   Traditional Reposado Tequila *(see recipe below)*
1/2 ounce Cointreau
1 ounce fresh squeezed lime juice
1 ounce simple syrup
Salt
Lime wedge

Cedar-Infused Tequila
1 (2 x 7-inch) cedar wood plank
1 bottle (750 ml.) Jose Cuervo Traditional Reposado

TIP
*Dissolve 2 parts sugar
into 1 part water
to make a
simple syrup.*

Combine all ingredients in a shaker glass or tin. Add ice to the shaker and shake until all ingredients are mixed well. Strain into a coupe glass and garnish with a half-salt rim and a lime wedge.

To make Cedar Infused Tequila, place the 2 x 7-inch cedar wood plank in a large jar and pour the bottle of Jose Cuervo Traditional Reposado tequila into the jar. Cover tightly with lid and let the cedar infuse the tequila for 4 days. After 4 days, finely strain the tequila and store, tightly covered, in a separate container.

TEXAS TEA

Grady's Restaurant, Fort Worth

Serves 6

3 ounces clear tequila
3 ounces Triple Sec
3 ounces white rum
3 ounces Tito's Texas Vodka
1 (12-ounce) can Sprite
1 (12-ounce) can Dr. Pepper

Fill 6 highball glasses ¾ full of ice. In a large shaker half filled with ice, add the tequila, Triple Sec, rum, and vodka. Shake well, then immediately strain and divide evenly into the highball glasses. Top each glass with a splash each of Dr. Pepper and Sprite and serve cold.

SITTIN' ON THE PORCH

Grady's Restaurant, Fort Worth

Serves 1

1 1/2 ounces Southern Comfort
1 ounce peach schnapps
1 ounce cranberry juice
1 lime wedge, for garnish

Fill a glass with ice. Add the Southern Comfort, schnapps and cranberry juice and stir. Squeeze the lime into the glass, drop it in, and enjoy while sittin' on the porch.

THE TEXICAN

Grady's Restaurant, Fort Worth

Serves 4

8 ounces clear tequila
12 ounces cranberry juice

6 teaspoons freshly squeezed lime juice
6 thinly-sliced lime rounds, for garnish

Fill 4 highball glasses ¾ full of ice. In a cocktail shaker half filled with ice, add the tequila, cranberry juice and lime juice. Shake until well combined, then strain and divide evenly into the highball glasses. Place a lime round on each glass and serve cold.

TEXAS LEMONADE

Grady's Restaurant, Fort Worth

Serves 1

1 wedge fresh lemon (for frosting
   the glass)
Granulated sugar (for frosting
   the glass)
1 ½ ounces Herradura white tequila
1 ounce freshly squeezed lemon juice
2 tablespoons super fine sugar
2 slices candied limes

Candied Limes
2 cups granulated sugar
1 1/2 cups water
3 limes, thinly sliced
2 tablespoons piloncillo (or,
   equal parts brown sugar
   and cinnamon)

Coat the rim of a large glass with the lemon wedge, then dip the rim into a plate of granulated sugar to frost. Fill the glass with ice. In a tumbler, combine tequila, lemon juice, and superfine sugar and stir until sugar dissolves. Strain into frosted glass and garnish with Candied Limes.

To make the Candied Limes, combine sugar and water in a saucepan over high heat. Bring the mixture to a boil, then reduce to a simmer. Add the lime slices and cook for 25 to 30 minutes until soft, with plenty of liquid remaining. Remove the pan from the heat and let cool 15 minutes. Transfer the limes to a plate and dust each slice with the piloncillo and let cool for 20 to 30 minutes. Stored at room temperature, these slices will keep for 4 to 5 days.

◦◦ INDEX ◦◦

ACKNOWLEDGMENTS

We are especially indebted to Grady Spears for agreeing to write the foreword for this book, and for his wonderful contribution of recipes; and to June Naylor for using her great knowledge of Texas restaurants to put together a delightful and definitive list of recipes.

Thanks also to the owners, managers, and chefs who endured repeated calls with questions and clarifications to their fabulous dishes; and to Patricia Sharpe, who is a bottomless well of information about Texas food and who is, thankfully, always willing to share her knowledge.